Heshel's Kingdom

Heshel's Kingdom

DAN JACOBSON

HAMISH HAMILTON · LONDON

HAMISH HAMILTON LTD

Published by the Penguin Group
Penguin Books Ltd, 27 Wrights Lane, London w8 5tz, England
Penguin Books USA Inc., 375 Hudson Street, New York, New York 10014, USA
Penguin Books Australia Ltd, Ringwood, Victoria, Australia
Penguin Books Canada Ltd, 10 Alcorn Avenue, Toronto, Ontario, Canada m4v 3b2
Penguin Books (NZ) Ltd, 182–190 Wairau Road, Auckland 10, New Zealand

Penguin Books Ltd, Registered Offices: Harmondsworth, Middlesex, England

First published 1998
1 3 5 7 9 10 8 6 4 2

Grateful acknowledgement is made to the Polish Cultural Foundation (London) for
permission to quote the lines from Kenneth Mackenzie's translation of *Pan Tadeusz* by
Adam Mickiewicz which appear on page 172

Set in 11.25/14pt Monotype Sabon
Typeset by Intype London Ltd
Printed in England by Clays Ltd, St Ives, plc

A CIP catalogue record for this book is available from the British Library

ISBN 0–241–13927–9

In the nation that is not
Nothing stands that stood before
A. E. HOUSMAN

Contents

Prologue

My childhood was spent in Kimberley, the diamond-mining town in South Africa.

In those years most of the mines were no longer being worked. They did not even have fences around them. You could, if you dared, go right to the edge of the two biggest open mines, the Kimberley Mine and the De Beers Mine, and look directly into the depths below. Their central pits were hundreds of feet across, thousands of feet in depth.

It was terrifying to stand above them. Yet from time to time I would feel compelled to do so. The contrast between the banality of the earth underfoot and the emptiness that yawned fatally from it, a single pace ahead, was irresistible. There was no compromise between the two. Only an edge. On this side, life. On that, its unimaginable opposite.

All of it man-made too. That was part of the fascination of these places. Everywhere else, flatness, flatness, flatness.

Later the pits were fenced in. After forty years of inactivity the search for diamonds in the De Beers Mine was resumed; the Kimberley Mine was turned into a tourist attraction. An open-air museum was established nearby. Only on the outskirts of town did a few smaller mines remain unfenced and unguarded. One of these was called Otto's Kopje. It had its own diminished version of an open pit and several vertical shafts at varying distances around it. The shafts did not have any broken ground near them to warn you of what was ahead. You just came upon them: perfectly square, black holes in the ground, each as big as a room, and apparently bottomless. At night, in bed, I would occasionally be racked out of sleep by a sudden involuntary step into that black space.

In early adulthood I left South Africa and went to live in England. There too, quite by chance, I was able to make solitary visits to various disused mine shafts. Near the house owned by my wife's father, in south Devon, were many acres of woodland riddled with disused copper-workings. These were much older than the mines in Kimberley; they had been abandoned decades before the opening of the diamond fields in 1870. Their shafts did not go down nearly as far as those I had looked into, or looked away from, in earlier years. But they too were cut square and were unfenced, half-hidden by overhanging fronds of bracken and branches of trees. Inside the shafts it was possible to make out a rough layer of clay and pebbles, like a thick skin; then, as one's eyes became accustomed to the darkness, a further level of hewn rock, the rough flanges of which seemed to reach out to one another, across the vacancies of the pit itself. Further down rock and emptiness merged into a gathering of shadows, visible as misty colours only – mauve, green, brown, blue. Below that, darkness. An absence of texture and colour. An absence of everything.

I could never visit one of these pits without looking for something to throw into it. Once I tossed in a book I had been carrying in my jacket pocket. Call it an act of literary criticism. Most of the objects – stones, lumps of earth, bits of branch – simply went straight down; others I would throw up in the air, for the pleasure of seeing how they appeared to hang momentarily over the middle of the shaft before falling.

Then I waited for the sound each made when it hit the bottom. The reverberations from below were sometimes no louder than a discreet cough; sometimes almost as loud as a train shunting. Occasionally I also heard sounds like chimes or cries.

Now try to imagine a man dropping a stone into a pit and waiting for a reverberation which never comes back to him, no matter how long he stands there. The thing that had been in his hand, that had hung briefly above the vacancy below, is dropping silently into a deeper silence. Let him leave the shaft, go elsewhere, sleep, work, eat, travel, watch television. The stone is falling still, dropping further and further from the square of darkness which had yawned under it, before being transformed instantly into a square of light receding above it. Dwindling rapidly in size from something like a room to a box, a book, a postcard, a stamp, a pinpoint, the light has long since vanished. Still the stone drops, never meeting any resistance, never producing the sound of having at last come to a halting place.

That is what the past is like: echoless and bottomless. Only its shallowest levels, those closest to us, have recognizable colours and forms. So we fix our gaze there. Below them is a darkness that gives back nothing.

PART ONE

Lithuania

[1]

Since I never met my grandfather, Rabbi Heshel Melamed, I never lost him. For me he has always been one of the dead. He has always belonged to that region where shadows give way to unchanging darkness. How could we have met? I was born more than a decade after his death, in a country he never visited.

In fact, if he had not died prematurely, I would never have been born.

No doubt many grandchildren could say the same about their grandfathers. Deaths occur, families move, as a result new connections are made, children are conceived who would not otherwise have come into existence.

In his case and mine, however, there lies between us the gulf of an unspeakable history.

Anyway, as the one who came later I have the advantage of him. I can speak of him and he cannot answer or put me right. At any moment the difference between us may be abolished. My silence will have become indistinguishable from his. Yet for the time being no difference could be greater; nothing can compare with it.

That is one advantage I have. Another is his ignorance of everything that has happened in the world since his death. I mean matters personal to him in the first place. He does not know, for example, what became of the widow he left behind;

3

or the nine children she had by him – whom they married, what work they did, where they lived, what children they in their turn had, how they died. I mean also world events, the imminence of which he had no inkling: wars, revolutions, migrations, massacres, proclamations of independence and so forth.

That is not all. I know just how those 'personal matters' and 'world events' merged into each other, in such a way that it is impossible for me or anyone else to tell them apart.

For all these reasons I know something else that would have seemed utterly grotesque to him, had anyone been able to say it to him during his last illness. I know that the kindest thing he did for his wife and children was to die quite suddenly, at the age of fifty-three, leaving them penniless and helpless.

Now there's a patrimony for them! For me! For all his grandchildren and great-grandchildren who live today in England, Israel, South Africa and the United States.

Nothing would be morally cheaper (tempting though it is) than for me to look back at the extent of his ignorance and to shake my head over the terrible mistakes of judgement he made. The fact that his mistakes were made in good faith, as people say – indeed, that they were made as an expression and demonstration of his faith, and in defiance of those who cared less about it than he did – appears to me ironic and pitiable. It also fills me, as a non-believer, with emotions much darker than these. How a believer would deal with such emotions, and the questions that lie behind them, I do not know.

But he died – luckily for himself, as things turned out, and for those immediately around him.

Please do not misunderstand me. I do not suppose that in some inconceivable afterlife Rabbi Yisrael Yehoshua Melamed, known to his wife as Heshel, can hear me and understand what I am saying. First of all, he is dead and my understanding of death is that it is death indeed: the end of consciousness for the person whose life has been extinguished. He may be remembered in whatever manner his descendants are able to do so, but that is their doing, the task and gift of the living, not of the dead.

Secondly, even when he was alive he did not speak English.

So why do I write of him? To show how much wiser about the world I am than he ever was?

Not at all. I take no credit for the accident of chronology. Rather, I want to look at it this way. Encoded in the loops of DNA in every cell of my body are discrete physical, mental and emotional potentialities which are my grandfather's as much as mine; mine because they were once his. The genes I have inherited from him cannot be changed or done away with; they were and are capable only of combining in unpredictable fashion with countless others from other sources. Some of those which he passed on to me have doubtless been 'expressed', as the geneticists say, this time around, my time around; I would see them in the mirror, if I knew where to look; I would recognize them, if only I knew how, in the states of mind they give rise to, in the sensations I experience, in the feelings which move me. In my habits of perception too. Other encoded potentialities, dormant in him, still dormant in me, wait to be summoned forth in other combinations and occasions, in persons still to be born.

The pit of the future is quite as deep as the pit of the past. Through it, too, all things fall endlessly. Genes included.

By evoking the shadow of my grandfather I hope to discover elements in his life and mine which are now hidden from me. Through him or with him I would like to find out, if I can, what we have in common and what we do not; how remote we are from one another and how close; in what terms it might be possible for me to put together all I already know about us both with everything I will never know. His life and his death (together!) were indispensable to my existence. Now I must try to make myself indispensable to his.

*

He is the only one of my grandparents I never met. Of the four of them he alone does not lie in the pale brown, quartzy soil of one or another of Johannesburg's Jewish cemeteries. When I think of the other three I face the stubbornly indisposable memory of their presence. But him? Heshel Melamed? He is a fateful absence, a bodiless name, hardly more. He has always been the one who owned death or was owned by it. The death of each of my other grandparents was different: each was an event, if only a remote one, in my life; known through a sequence of letters, telephone calls, parents' emotions and journeys, which I remember not so much as a loss of my own but as one belonging to an adulthood I had yet fully to enter.

Heshel Melamed was different, however. He still is. Death, closure, 'existlessness' (Thomas Hardy's word) was always his lot. When I was a child this rendered him peculiarly distant and mysterious. Now that I am so much older, he has become far closer to me than he was then. The corridors of thought which lead to him are shorter than they used to be. He, who stood behind my coming-into-being, now waits for my ceasing-to-be. He is the expert on both conditions. His is the absence into which my absence will eventually be absorbed.

As a little boy I believed that he died because his 'blood had turned to water'. I understood this phrase in the most literal fashion. No doubt I had misheard something said by the adults. The idea of it, of the magical chemistry involved in such a death, was a source of worry to me. Could it happen to anyone? Could it happen to me? Was it the consequence perhaps of drinking too much water? Or of not drinking enough? Did the red fluid inside him actually become as thin and transparent as water? I did not dare to ask any of these questions aloud, for fear of being laughed at, but I turned them around in my mind.

Now I know better. The truth must have been the exact opposite of my fantasy. So far from his blood turning to water, it must have thickened into clots which attached themselves to the walls of his arteries. One seizure was followed by another until all was over with him.

That, more or less, was what happened to his oldest daughter, my mother. It had already happened at a much earlier age to one of her younger sisters, Rae. I was not with my mother when she died, but I was on a visit home when she suffered her penultimate heart attack, a few months before the end. How she laboured for breath! How bright and wide open her brown eyes were, staring from below! The ambulance men carried her out of the house on a stretcher covered with blue blankets. She was supine. She saw me leaning over the stretcher, but could not speak. It was as if my presence told her only how much closer she now was to her father than she was to me. How little chance she and I had of reaching each other.

It was just before sunrise, on a morning no different from any other. Except for what was happening to her.

She was sixty-seven years old then, exactly as old as I am now. No angioplasty for her. No triple-bypass operation. Such procedures were not known in those days. All they could do, once she had been taken into hospital, was to cover her nose and mouth with an oxygen mask. Would clot-busting drugs have been available at that time in a small-town hospital like the one in Kimberley? I doubt it.

So what chance did he have, in Varniai (Vorna to him), Lithuania, forty years before? With the same ailment? In 1919, less than a year after the end of the First World War?

I once asked my mother if her father had believed in an afterlife. Did he think that the soul of a pious Jew like himself would survive to enjoy some kind of transcendental existence in another world? Remarkably enough, given the position he occupied as rabbi and leader of the community in the *shtetl* in which he lived, she answered, 'I really don't know. I don't know what he thought about that.'

Evidently the issue was not clear cut enough, or perhaps not important enough, for him to have made his attitude to it plain, even to those closest to him. This may reveal something about him (e.g. that there was perhaps a stronger vein of scepticism running through his belief than I am able to grasp). It certainly tells us something about how indeterminate Judaism has allowed itself to be about doctrines with which Christianity has always been centrally preoccupied. In the Hebrew Scriptures allusions to the afterlife are few and far between. Later the idea of the survival of the individual soul did become embedded in the Jewish liturgy and in the writings of the rabbis. But I have the impression that even there it remained secondary in importance to the immortality of the peoplehood of Israel.

His personal immortality (or mine) hardly mattered at all, compared to that of the people as a whole. As individuals we would have nothing to complain about, provided the children of Israel at last achieved the unimaginable reward promised to them, in the equally unimaginable messianic age.

There is just one photograph of Heshel Melamed in my possession. It is in front of me now. It is not large – about six inches by four inches – and is printed in the sepia tints of the time. It remains strikingly clear and unfaded, however, given that it is about ninety years old. Taken from the front, though not directly so, it shows his head and shoulders only, with a top hat affixed above. Because it reaches to such a height, and because of the elaborate curl of its brim, the hat is as prominent as anything else in the picture. Its salience is emphasized also by a highlight that runs vertically from the band above the brim to a vanishing point just right of centre.

Nothing else in the photo is as bright as that bar of light; not even the two smaller highlights shining within his wide-open eyes. Shaped like a French circumflex gone slightly awry, each shows up as a tiny white gleam just above his black pupils.

Looking at them I can still see today, reflected in his eyes, the light that once shone in some photographic studio in Kaunas (Kovno to him) or Siauliai (Shavel to him). The reflections bear indubitable witness to the consciousness that was then his. Obedient to the photographer's command, he had self-consciously stiffened his gaze and directed it into the black lens of his camera. Focusing at that point, he was aware too, though much more fuzzily, of the brass rim and wooden casing around the lens.

I speak so confidently of what he saw then because I know about that kind of camera. They are only to be found in museums now; but when I was a boy in Kimberley there was a photographer in town who still used one of them. From time to time my father and mother dressed up themselves and their four children to have photographs of the family, individually and collectively, taken by him. Because he was of 'diminished growth', I remember, he did not crouch as other photographers did in order to get under his black cloak and look through the aperture. He had to stand on a special box to get there.

That is not all I see, or find myself remembering, as I look into this representation of my grandfather's gleaming eyes, which is as faithful as the technology of the time could make it. In and through his eyes, and beyond them, I see my mother's eyes too. His have the same shape as hers; the same curvature of the eyeball; the same structure of surrounding bone into which it fits. Like his, her eyes were brown and exceptionally bright: brightest of all, as I have just said, when she was carried on a stretcher out of the house in Kimberley.

What else does the photograph show? Cheekbones also deeply familiar to me: not from my mother in this case, but from her siblings. A straight, shapely nose. A clear skin. A black, full beard with a grey tinge and an upward curl at the edges. A moustache, still wholly black, conceals most of his upper lip.

Where his beard mingles with the hair of his head (no dangling ringlets of a fanatical, Hasidic kind for him), one ear emerges clearly. The other is all but hidden. It is thus apparent that the photographer has chosen to stand slightly to one side of him.

A fragment of black bow tie can be seen just beneath his beard; below that is a small, triangular section of white shirting. The rest of him, or what is shown of him, is clad in a black frock coat. Only one of its lapels is on view; also one arm, two large buttons, several creases.

His expression is severe, I would say, but not unkind.

Looking more closely at this picture than I have ever done before, I realize something else about 'our relationship' I had not previously understood. Because he died more than ten years before I was conceived, I have always, in quasi-instinctive fashion, thought of him as someone older than myself. Permanently older, I mean. Born older, living older, dying older.

In fact, when this picture was taken he was much younger than I am now. So far from being my reverend senior, he was my junior. Now. Then too.

[2]

The occasion for the taking of this photograph was Heshel Melamed's forthcoming departure for the United States. He made the journey in 1912, seven years before his death, eight years before his widow and her children sailed for South Africa.

It is a true portrait, however; no passport job. A fine one, too, in its sharpness of outline and expressiveness of gaze. Look at the crisp curl of the beard, the clarity of the line of his nostrils. And those alert eyes, to which I cannot stop myself returning. The picture was taken, I have no doubt, in a *nunc dimittis* spirit: as a pre-journey act, a gesture towards the future, a way of leaving something of himself behind. How could the hazards of travel which lay ahead, and the uncertainty of events at home, not have been at work in his brain? And not only in his brain but elsewhere too: producing hollow pangs in his stomach, a tightness in his chest, a faintness in his head.

He was to go all the way (and his address book, which I also have, provides the evidence of it) from Varniai to Cleveland, Ohio – and back. Or not, as fate and God and he himself would eventually decide. First he would travel by train (with several changes) to Hamburg; then by steamer to New York, to stay with relations of his wife's in Brownsville; then once more by train to Cleveland, where, it had been suggested, he might become the rabbi of a community of Lithuanian Jews (Litvaks) who had established themselves there. *En route* he would also be making calls in Newark, New Jersey, and in Akron, Ohio, where other *landsleit* and members of the family had established themselves.

A big deal, a step into a strange world. I am not tempted to patronize him for what he felt about it; all else aside, I remember too clearly my own alarm and excitement when, at the age of twenty, I stepped into an aeroplane for the first time in my life. Like him, I was leaving the country of my birth, also for the first time. (An old tin tub of a Dakota the plane was, discharged from service once the Second World War had come to its end, several years before.)

He knew Hebrew, he knew Yiddish, he was able, as a speaker of Yiddish, to make himself understood in German; he had more than a few phrases of Lithuanian and Russian as well. Now he was about to enter another world, one filled with speakers of Polish, French, Dutch, English and God alone knew what other Babel-born tongues. To be a bearded, top-hatted, frock-coated rabbi 'at home' in Lithuania was to be conscious of estrangement and exile, local hostility (sometimes) and legally enforced restriction (always). Nevertheless he regarded himself, and took it for granted that he should be regarded by others, as the most important figure in the Jewish community of Varniai; even the gentiles agreed in assigning that position to him. His people deferred to him and respected the rulings he issued to them on innumerable personal and religious problems. He was the head of his own large household and, the obscurity of his own background notwithstanding, he was connected by marriage with one of the most distinguished rabbinical families in the province. (Or so its members liked to believe.) The fields of Lithuania may have been those of exile; but he had never walked on any other. The country's soft but distant horizons had surrounded him from his infancy. The pattern of its woodlands, marshes and fallow spaces was imprinted on his eye and mind. The shape of its low, wooden houses was as familiar to him as the ever-fading, ever-cracking hues of blue, green and yellow in which they were painted. In Varniai he instinctively took his bearings, whether or not he was conscious of doing so, by the town's high-towered, modestly domed churches; he measured the passing of the day by the sound of their bells. When he travelled to other towns he knew as if by instinct who and what were to be avoided – and when; who was to be placated – and how; where, among his fellow Jews, shelter and succour would be found. All over the country, not to speak of cities like Vilnius (Vilna to him) and Kaunas, the Jews made up such a large proportion of the population – in some areas almost as much as a half of it – he was confident he would never want for a welcome among them.

But out there? In Poland and Germany, which he would have to cross by rail? In a ship sailing the mighty ocean? In the New World?

Ninety years later, looking at this studio portrait, which – along with a Russian identity document, his address book and the case in which he kept his spectacles – remains his sole, external, material legacy, I have to admire his steadiness of gaze, the seriousness of his expression, the determination he shows to confront and discharge his responsibilities. His lower lip makes no attempt to curve itself into anything as frivolous as a smile. It is not his business to ingratiate himself with the photographer in front of him, or with anyone who may look at the man's work five or ten or a hundred years later; he offers no excuses or palliations-in-advance for what he is or what he does, or how he will cope with the discomforts and misfortunes that may lie ahead. Nor is there the faintest evidence in his gaze of a self-protective irony.

At the same time, despite the steadiness of that gaze, his eyes betray to mine an undergleam of vulnerability. Perhaps I see it

13

there because his eyes are so much like my mother's: the very first eyes I ever looked into; the first to look into mine.

I turn now to the other relics mentioned a moment ago. First, his address book. It is pocket-size and is covered in a black, slippery, shiny material, a kind of primitive plastic. (Can it be what used to be called 'American leather'?) From the fact that almost all the names and addresses in it are of people in various cities in the United States, I infer that it was specially bought for his American journey. Most of the entries are in ink; a few are in pencil. The hand that made them appears to be unskilled in writing the Roman script: the individual letters and the joins between them have a spacious yet curiously unconvincing look. No other graphological clues emerge from them. Each of the entries is particular, it refers to a specific person, yet taken together, as the brittle pages whisper and shiver under my fingers, they create an effect of a generalized pathos: lives gone, connections lost, tongues fallen silent, buildings in all likelihood long since demolished. Time displayed at its usual relentless work; bringing us into being, sending us into oblivion.

The book also has some notes and names in the cursive Hebrew script, most of which are indecipherable to me, and many anxious calculations of a financial kind: little multiplications and subtractions and additions of what I take to be roubles, dollars, marks – who can tell? Times of train connections appear too, with names of stations and railroad companies attached. None of the people he was hoping to visit had telephone numbers, so far as I can make out. Obscure smudges appear here and there (did he wet his forefinger as he turned over the pages?), as well as one large stain (tea, coffee?) shaped like a country I have never seen on any map.

Next, his spectacles case. In the photograph he is not wearing spectacles, but I know from my mother that he was short-sighted and usually wore them in 'real life'. That is, when not standing rigid before a camera.

My mother was myopic too. So am I. So is my daughter.

The case is covered in leather which is chipped away in places, so that the dull, pewter-coloured metal beneath is revealed. Its hinges are very stiff. The lining inside is of some coarse-fibred cloth, like calico; but a piece of faded, broken silk, no doubt used for cleaning the lenses, also lies in the case.

On that strip of silk, like an Egyptian corpse in its sarcophagus, the spectacles rest where they were left. They are motionless. Their arms are folded behind them. Only their lenses – small, thick, oval in shape, set in frames of gilded metal – seem to stir in the light (from another age) that now falls on them.

My hands hesitate, as a grave robber's might. I have to summon my will to pick up the glasses and take them out of the case, which at once snaps shut with a surprisingly loud noise: a miniature, resonant, guilt-inducing clang. Unfolding the metal shafts, I fit the springy ends of coiled wire over my ears, adjust the little arch on the bridge of my nose and look up.

The result is awful – something worse than blindness, a turmoil of curved stripes, blurred spaces, dwindling verticals, mad gleams in corners. A place of nausea; vertigo; parody.

So this is what his world looked like!

It may well be that no one else has looked through these spectacles since he used them last. Since his death, in fact, just about eighty years ago.

There is something uncanny in the thought. It has a vertigo of its own.

He sickened and weakened rapidly, suffered one 'episode' after another, and died at home. That much I know. Varniai had a doctor (a gentile, according to my aunt Sadie), but it was too small a town to have a hospital, and it would have been cruel as well as costly to transport him fifty miles over poor roads to Siauliai, where there must have been a hospital of some kind. (Of what kind?) Even more unthinkable was the prospect of then putting him on a train and sending him a further hundred miles south-east to Kaunas. Or west to Klaipeda (Memel, as he would have called it). And how much would he have been helped if they had done so? Consider how little my mother was helped in the Kimberley Hospital during her last illness, after forty-five years of medical advance and with financial resources at her disposal that would have seemed breathtakingly lavish to her father.

During his last illness these glasses lay on a table next to his bed, or on a chest of drawers nearby. We all leave our glasses in such places, when lying in bed. After the funeral his widow put them aside, along with a few other items she prized especially because of their intimacy with him. When the family's meagre possessions were packed up for the great migration to South Africa she took them with her: mute memorials of an exhausted life, of a marriage transformed into nothing more than the dark holes and sudden incandescences of memory. For the next thirty years she kept them with her. In addition to the photograph (then in a brown wooden frame) and his identity document, address book and spectacles, I can remember her once showing me an umbrella and a leather-bound *machzor* or prayer book which she said were his. Only the first four items were still in her possession when she died. After her death they came into my mother's hands, and after her death into mine, as a result of my brothers and sister jointly agreeing that my methodical wife should be made family archivist and curator.

That is how Heshel Melamed's glasses come to be on my desk now, lying where they were flung down after I had torn them off my face. They gaze trustfully up at me, in slightly lopsided fashion. Though I feel a qualm of nausea at the thought of looking through them again, the temptation to do it is too strong to be resisted.

So close he is. So distant and indifferent.

Very well then.

The shock of the bulging, cavorting, caving-in, rainbow-coloured disorder I look into is not diminished. Nor is the relief I feel on tearing the apparatus off my face – so violently this time that I scratch the skin behind my right ear.

For me it is a kind of torture to look at the world through his spectacles. For him they made his world habitable. They gave clear outline to its shapes; detail and colour to the faces of his children and neighbours; access to the books of the Torah and to the talmudic commentaries he studied, discussed and preached from. The idea of anything uncanny or repellent inhering in these utilitarian lenses and frames would have seemed outlandish to him. They were for unfolding and putting on; for removing from his nose and from behind his ears (without scratching himself); for folding up and putting into their case.

Nothing else. Nor would it have occurred to him that they would outlast him by so many decades; that they would be carried to South Africa – of all places! – by his widow; and later still carried back to Europe by a granddaughter-in-law.

He was paid so little as rabbi of the largest *shul* in Varniai that a special arrangement had been made to enable his wife to earn a few extra coppers. She enjoyed the monopoly of selling yeast to the other Jewish householders in town (including those who attended its two other, much smaller, synagogues).

Imagine the turnover this enterprise engendered! Imagine the humiliation for her – and him – in having to eke out the family income in this fashion!

That was one of the reasons why he went to the United States.

He had an irritably exalted idea of his learning and intellectual capabilities. He also knew exactly what the prospects were for him and his family as long as he remained in a backward little town like Varniai: 'remote, out-of the-way, lacking streets and convenient transportation to the central cities of the country', as it was to be described many years later by two conscientious encyclopedists of such communities. Some of his wife's relations, rabbis among them, had migrated to the United States during the previous decade or two. From there they had sent home offers of help and occasional small sums of money. Why should he not join them? Why not seize the chance to establish himself in America, where many groups of recently arrived Litvaks were looking for rabbis who would help them re-create a semblance of the life they had known in *der heim*?

So he had his photograph taken and bought a new outfit, a new notebook, a new portmanteau and the fateful tickets. Four months in all he was to be away – one month coming and going, more or less; three months travelling in America.

With some fellow-feeling, and a touch of *schadenfreude*, I think of him travelling on his own across half of Europe, over the Atlantic, in and out of a half-dozen North American cities and across the spaces between them: alone, unknown, disregarded, frequently depressed and homesick, filled with the anxieties all travellers know, in addition to some particular to someone like himself, who could never forget for a moment the dietary regulations to which he was bound and the demands of the many Sabbaths and the few festivals which would occur while he was away. I see him standing on street corners or outside railroad stations in pre-First World War American cities, his umbrella in one hand and his brass-locked, loaf-shaped, leather portmanteau at his feet: a stubby, formal, buttoned-up, bewhiskered figure in his middle forties; the father of at least six children by then (with another no doubt already on the way); given to sleeplessness (my mother suffered from it too) and indigestion (his son Michael was to be another victim of that ailment). Footsore, buffeted by strangers, waiting in unfamiliar places for cousins or *landsleit* whose faces he is not sure he will recognize, he puts his hand to his breast pocket to make sure that the hard, reassuring bulge of his wallet and address book is still there. As he does it a feeling of excessive fatigue surprises him. So does an unexplained ache in the chest and across his shoulders (presaging the illness which is going to kill him a few years hence).

Now he boards a train or streetcar. Later, adjusting his spectacles on the bridge of his nose, he sits in a Jewish boarding house and writes a letter home, or perhaps one to the next family he hopes to visit on his travels. Here in his address book I see a Finestein in Brooklyn; there a Levy upstate in Albany; here a Pulvermacher in Cincinnati.

How comfortable and secure his home back in Varniai must have seemed in comparison with all this! And how bruisingly distant! Like every other malady, homesickness cares nothing for time or, strangely enough, for persons. Those who suffer know *it*, all right, each in his or her own terms, but for its part the condition inhabits them as indifferently as a bacterium or virus. Hence the effects it produces are always much the same. Button your coat up still more tightly, Heshel Melamed, adjust your hat, look around you as severely as possible: nothing you do hides from onlookers and passers-by the vulnerability of the figure you cut. Your hands are soft; your gaze is a newcomer's; your posture a scholar's. No wonder some of the urchins in the street feel free to jostle you and shout 'Sheeny Viskers!' in your ear – an unfamiliar, even exotic, insult which you will report to your family, when you get safely home.

Decades later, in Kimberley, South Africa, his oldest daughter will repeat this insult in telling me about his journey. There is no outrage in her tone: only sadness and, in spite of herself, a certain mild amusement.

*

19

Anyway, when he got home he had worse things than the insults of urchins to report to his family about the New World, this golden America, this land for evermore-about-to-be which had supposedly cast off ancient Europe's hatreds and cruelties. It was not the grossness and hostility of the gentiles that had shocked him there. What else could be expected of them? Wherever the Jews came on them – and that was everywhere – they would find much the same sort of thing, sooner or later. In Lithuania too there were plenty of people ready to use foul words to them, in a language that the victims understood well enough, and to make threatening gestures at them.

No, it wasn't the children shouting 'Sheeny Viskers!' after him in the streets that decided him never to return to the United States. Nor was it because so few words of the language spoken there were comprehensible to him. Nor because he found the country overwhelmingly huge and populous to a degree for which nothing in his previous experience had prepared him. None of that. What made the United States uninhabitable, as far as he was concerned, had nothing to do with what the gentiles got up to. It was the degradations the Jews inflicted on themselves there that were intolerable to him.

That, essentially, was his view of the United States. He came back to Varniai and reported that once they had landed there all but a tiny number of the Jewish immigrants forsook the ways of their forefathers and the laws of Moses. They shaved their beards; they worked on the Sabbath as if it were a day like any other; they attended *shul* rarely; they ate forbidden foods; their women wore indecent clothes; they gave up saying the prayers that should have accompanied their daily actions – rising, washing the hands, eating, leaving the home, retiring to sleep. Worse still, perhaps, was the contempt with which such people, some of whom had been in the country for a few years only, had taken to speaking of those like himself who clung to the old ways, to the ways God had laid down for them. If that was how the new arrivals behaved, what would become of their children in a place like that? And their children's children? What abominations would they commit?

Yes, an appointment had been offered to him in some dingy, noisy quarter of Cleveland; but no, he had not been tempted to take it up. Life in Varniai was poor and uncomfortable: that he knew. For reasons he could never understand he was apparently condemned to remain the rabbi of a *shtetl* inhabited largely by ignoramuses and paupers. (His words for them, in his darker moods.) But if that was the price he had to pay for preserving everything he most valued, so be it. At least he knew that he was keeping himself, his wife and his children safe from the corruptions and contaminations that threatened them elsewhere.

Here in Lithuania he would never be alone, not even in his poverty. He would continue to take his modest place among the generations of scholars and pious rabbis who had made the country's name a byword all over Jewish Europe for austere devotion and intellectual rigour. Some of his predecessors had established famous *yeshivas* (talmudic seminaries) and houses of study in cities like Kaunas and Vilnius and Telz; others had lived and died in towns only a little bigger, or even smaller, than the one in which he served. They had not been fanatics; nor did he ever think of himself as one. He despised the outlandish garb and messianic antics of the Hasidim: a sect which had come into existence precisely as an act of rebellion against the traditions of book-bound learning to which he attached so great an importance. He regarded it as an honour to bear the title given to those who were unremittingly hostile to the Hasidic movement: he was a *mitnagid*, an opponent. He was contemptuous too of the political activism of the Zionists, who imagined that they could re-establish the people of Israel in the promised land without God's help. He knew that the people of Israel would earn their redemption, however long it might be deferred, in one way only: not by crossing the seas and adopting the ways of the gentiles in distant continents, but by prayer, study, teaching, preaching, the observation of every biblical commandment and every rabbinical injunction to its last insignificant and mighty letter.

[3]

That was how he spoke about America after his return to his wife, his older children, his in-laws, the Jews of the town. I had my mother's word for it, many years later, thousands of lucky miles from Lithuania.

'What about you?' I asked. 'Were you disappointed that you weren't going to America?'

She pressed her hands together in a manner she sometimes had: not at all beseechingly, but rather as if a remote or difficult truth would emerge from the pressure she was putting on them.

'I think I was a little disappointed. Probably I was relieved too. Anyway, it was what father had decided, so that was that.'

Not that he found everything to his liking when he got back to his brick-walled, wooden-verandaed house in Varniai. (It was then the only brick-built house in Varniai, my mother told me; the only double-storeyed one too. Half of it, however, was owned by, or perhaps let to, the cantor of his synagogue.)

Soon after his return he discovered, by chance, that his wife, Menuchah, had managed to get hold of a German translation of Erenst Renan's *Vie de Jésus*, which she had been reading in her spare time.

My mother did not know how the book had come into her mother's possession. She guessed that it had been borrowed from someone in the town or that Menuchah had brought it back from one of her visits to Siauliai or Kelme (Kelm to him). Or the provincial capital Rasenai, perhaps.

There it was, anyway, this triply heretical item. First, it was a book about Jesus, of all people; second, it was in one of the gentile languages (Russian and German) for the literatures of which his wife had a deplorable fondness; third, it was notorious for being 'atheistical' in tendency.

So after a row which spoiled the homecoming for him and everyone else, he seized the offending book and carried it at arm's length out of the house and across the little front yard. Watched in silence by his wife, the children and the Lithuanian maid, Annele by name, he threw it into the road. The book flew through the air, its pages open and fluttering, and fell face-down in the mud.

It was raining at the time. It had rained the previous night too. The road was 'all mud', according to my mother. Yet he would not let Menuchah go out and pick it up. 'He grabbed her, he held her by both arms,' my mother said. 'She tried to get away but he was much stronger than she was.'

She had never seen her parents behave in this manner before. None of the children dared to go out and rescue the book. It lay where it had fallen.

'The next morning – well, you can imagine the state it was in. There was nothing left of it; nothing you could read.'

What followed was that which follows all serious marital rows: a sense of mutual betrayal and injury; solitary starings out of windows; retreats to darkened rooms; children with lowered voices and miserable, alert eyes; the mechanical performance of whatever domestic or public duties had to be done; the spiritless contemplation by husband or wife of a future which appeared to promise nothing but more of the same, indefinitely. There had always been a kind of warfare between him and his wife. Menuchah's habit of reading books – novels and other items – in Russian and German, and her eagerness to see her children follow her example, had been just one of the fronts they fought over. He demanded of himself and of everyone else in the family and his congregation the utmost strictness in the practice of their religion; whereas she – the *rebbitzen*, the rabbi's wife, herself the daughter of a rabbi, granddaughter of a rabbi, great-granddaughter of a rabbi – was as sceptical about the religion, and as recalcitrant in carrying out the duties around the home that it demanded of her, as she dared to be. She was ready, also, to let her children know how she felt. The two of them were always 'wrangling' about it, according to my mother.

It amazed me to hear this from her. The grandmother I knew, and whom I saw about twice a year on family visits to Johannesburg, could hardly have been more devout. She was so devout, in fact, that our home in Kimberley was effectively barred to her. In all the years of my childhood and adolescence, she visited us just once, for two or three days only; and that was it. During her visit she lived, so far as I could see, on boiled eggs cooked in a little pan which she had brought with her. (All the other utensils in the house were *treif* – unusable, not kosher.) Not even the birth of my baby sister, or the barmitzvahs of myself and my brothers, had been enough of an attraction to lure her back.

But when I said something like this to my mother she answered impatiently, 'Oh, she was always perverse!'

Perverse? My quiet, undemanding, sombrely clad grand-mother? To me she looked as if she had gone to a kind of finishing school – *finishing* school, indeed – where they taught old women the arts and necessities of grandmotherhood. How to shrink in height, lose weight, develop deep wrinkles, grow larger joints. How to bow the shoulders, lower the head, subdue the gestures, soften the voice. How to wear black skirts and jackets with white blouses, live alone in a single room, eat tiny meals and deploy a range of small, self-deprecatory gestures and facial expressions. How to keep in their place – mantelpiece, table, windowsill, bathroom ledge – many valueless, small objects.

No doubt my view of her was affected more than I realized by the stories I read and the movies I watched. In effect I was doing my best to make her over into some kind of traditional, storybook grandmother, with Jewish orthodox, immigrant trimmings attached. The fussiness of her religion, its innumerable injunctions about diet and domestic ceremonial, not to mention synagogue attendance, struck me as wholly appropriate to an aged widow who had never adjusted and never would adjust to the loss of her 'old country' and to the acquisition of a new one.

Much of this, I was to learn from my mother, was no more than my own fanciful yet wholly conventional reading of her character. I learned that as a married woman she had tried to test to the limit what might be permissible for someone in her position to do and to say, to read and to think. Only after she had been widowed – that is, only after her husband's attempts to dominate her had been brought to an end for ever and she herself was settled in naked, half-pagan South Africa – only then did she choose to become everything he had always wished her to be.

Perverse, indeed.

So far as I know none of Menuchah's children ever reproached her for the arduously pious mode of life she now pursued, though among themselves they made no attempt to hide the fatigued irritation with which they regarded it. If in Lithuania she had hankered after a world in which doubt and scepticism were values rather than vices, why did she not take advantage of the opportunities to explore them which were now offered her in go-ahead Johannesburg? Or if in her heart she had always been a true believer, then why had she not settled down to living like one in benighted Varniai? Then she would have made her husband a happier man and her household a more peaceful place.

But no, that would also have made things too easy for them both. Always she had to be out of step: a quasi-freethinker when an unquestioning orthodoxy was expected of her; a *frume*, a zealot, when she was free to be otherwise.

Yet I suspect that there was something else between herself and her husband which was known to them throughout their marriage, and not forgotten by her in the many years of her widowhood.

My mother occasionally spoke of her father as 'kind'; more often she and the others used words like 'strict', 'severe' and 'distant' about him. Occasionally I felt that she and her siblings were rather proud of having a father about whom such stiff-sounding words could be used. Distance and severity fitted the prominent position which he had held in the community; having a father with such manners and characteristics fed their consciousness of being descended from superior stock. Nevertheless, hidden within Heshel Melamed's marriage to Menuchah were some facts that were evidently so painful to her, and hence to her children, that they were barely able to speak about them. This applied to my mother too, who was a reticent person and yet also naively frank by nature. I doubt if she referred more than half a dozen times, and then only in the most truncated way, to these matters. From my uncles and aunts I heard even less about them.

For one thing, he had been married before. For another, during his prior marriage he had gone by a name different from the one by which his children knew him – and hence knew themselves. And even before that, as I have only recently discovered from the Schoenburgs' indispensable *Lithuanian Jewish Communities*, he appears to have borne yet another name.

At birth he was apparently registered as Pohan or Fohan.

Subsequently, under the name of Segal, he served for several years as the rabbi of Tryskiai (Trishick), a town even smaller and more inconsequential than Varniai. He was known as Segal still when he moved to the latter place to become rabbi there. Only on marrying Menuchah did he take the name of Melamed. Now, did he become 'Melamed' (meaning teacher) as a sign to his second wife and his second set of in-laws that he had put all his previous commitments behind him? Or were these three changes of name merely the consequence of illicit pieces of paperwork that enabled him to escape conscription into the Tsarist army? Or was there some other reason for them?

I have no idea.

Within my grandfather's severities and austerities, therefore, or his children's talk of them, there remain some puzzles. Within the passionate upholder of tradition they spoke of, the outline of an interloper, a changeling, a man with a doubtful past can perhaps be discerned. Of his first marriage nothing is known: not even by my last surviving aunt, who could tell me nothing about it when I questioned her just a few months ago. Not the name of his first wife, nor where she came from, nor where he married her, nor how long the marriage lasted, nor whether it was death or divorce which parted them. Was he a widower when he met Menuchah? Or had he sent his first wife away? Or did she leave of her own accord? If so, did she leave with another man, back in Tryskiai? Had his behaviour, his 'severity' and 'distance', driven her back to her parents' home? Had there been children by that marriage? Did my mother have half-brothers or half-sisters she knew nothing about?

The most likely answer to the last two questions must be no. Varniai was too small a town, and Tryskiai insufficiently distant from it (I would guess), for the existence of children by his first wife to have remained hidden. Still, the family silence on the matter – a silence more eloquent in its way than words themselves could be – suggests a strain on the subject between man and wife, and between the married couple and their children; it suggests how much difficulty Menuchah may have had in reconciling herself to her status as the second wife. Especially if she was of a rebellious and freethinking temperament (within the limits of the time and place, and her position). Who was this man, this change-of-name artist, ex-lover and ex-husband of another woman, to preach to her about piety and propriety? To tell her what she should think, how she should behave, what books she should read?

The only person I can remember ever breaking the silence about my grandfather's first marriage was my father; and even he did it only after my mother's death. During the years of his protracted widowerhood he took to speaking in more and more embittered fashion about the family he had married into. He never saw any of his in-laws during the last decades of his life, but this did not dim the ancient, fictitious, yet deeply felt grievances he harboured against them. His father-in-law included, even though the latter had died long before my father had met his oldest daughter.

Now, alone in what had been the matrimonial home, with his wife dead and his children long resident elsewhere, my father insisted to me that there had always been something 'shady' about Heshel Melamed. There were mysteries in his life, he claimed, of an unsavoury sort. His journey to the United States had not been made in search of honourable employment, but because he was compelled to go there. Perhaps it was because he had some kind of 'funny business' to transact with that 'other woman'. Or perhaps there was a claim on him from the child or children he had had by her. And why had he changed his name all of a sudden? Could the Tsarist police have been after him for fraud or bigamy? Or both? Was that it?

'That man,' he said to me, 'was a crook. A piece of upper-class rubbish.'

'Upper class' was an expression of my father's lingering respect, despite himself, for Heshel Melamed's rabbinical status; he was always acutely conscious, in his relations with my mother, of coming from a family which could claim no scholars among its members. 'Rubbish' needs no gloss. The combination of the two terms as a description of the grandfather I had never seen was so ludicrous I could not help laughing when I heard it.

My father responded with a look of anger and self-pity: a mixture of emotions that was as familiar to me as the posture he had assumed in his armchair. As familiar as the armchair itself, and the angle at which he had set it to the rest of the room.

If my father was right, however, and Heshel Melamed's mid-life change of name and wife shows that there was something awkward, if not 'shady', about his past, then some of his spiritual severities may have sprung precisely from his consciousness of having a past to live down; of needing to prove his worthiness to his wife and children, to the people of Varniai and to his new wife's family, those stuck-up Oppenheims of Kelme.

In which case he too was double-hearted and double-minded, in his own way. Maybe, *mon grandpère* was my *mon semblable* as well. This thought rouses not so much a feeling of intimacy with him as a strange envy. Given my own readiness to 'see both sides of the question', the difficulty I sometimes have in standing my own ground, or even in knowing whether it is ground I stand on or merely intellectual quicksand, I wonder what it would be like to crush one's self-divisions as successfully as he apparently did and to turn them all into obstinacy, self-assurance, severity, devotion to the rabbinic law, faith in God.

So I come again to what is probably the greatest of the differences between myself and my unknown grandfather. I mean his faith and my lack of it, the inability I have to believe in anything resembling the God he worshipped. With regard to his God, whether as a remote idea or an everyday reality, my scepticism is so profound, I am confronted or affronted by so many moral and intellectual difficulties, I hardly know where to begin in speaking of them. It is not the case that I think of Heshel Melamed's faith as mere superstition or folly, or that I regard my inability to share it as an infallible reflection of the deepest of truths about the universe. Yet as far back as I can remember, the more amazing the world struck me as being, the less plausibly could I imagine it to be the handiwork of a sentient, prescient spirit whose nature and purposes were cognate in any way with my own. With even more difficulty (if that is possible) could I conceive of a creator who would go to the trouble of creating the universe and peopling it with creatures like ourselves, and then choose to reveal versions of his name and moral nature at particular moments in history and not at others; to particular tribes or nations and not to others; in particular geographical locations and not in others.

All that, of course, being quite beside the problem of theodicy – the vindicating of an omnipotent deity, capable of reason, susceptible to feeling, supposedly the source of all good, worthy of our prayers and praise, who yet permits unmerited suffering to fall on creatures so much weaker and humbler than himself. Deer or mice, for instance; let alone children. Any children. Anywhere. At any moment in history.

There it is then. The gulf between myself and my rabbinical grandfather is not to be easily crossed: certainly not by glib talk of his beliefs as a kind of 'metaphor' for my scepticism. Or vice versa. Metaphors were hardly his business.

At the same time I do not want to make his manner of holding to his beliefs seem simpler than it was. I am sure that he frequently and directly questioned God's actions and was filled with pain and bewilderment over them. Why, for instance, had he inflicted so long and painful an exile on his people? And why had he consigned Heshel Melamed to a nothing of a place like Varniai? And so forth.

He felt no guilt or anxiety, no disloyalty either, in reproaching the God of Israel as fiercely as circumstances demanded. As fiercely as he deserved. Rebuking or even hectoring God on personal and national grounds had in itself been one of the faith's inveterate practices, from the days of the prophets onwards.

So the faith lived in Heshel Melamed. He lived in it. There was no point at which he ended and the other began.

[4]

I must have been six or seven years old when my mother told me a story about her childhood which for some reason I was never to forget. Perhaps it was because the story touched directly on feelings familiar to me; yet it approached them from the opposite direction to my own. She was the oldest of the children in her family; I was the youngest of three sons, with a sister much younger than myself. As a result I often felt envious of the privileges and advantages my older brothers enjoyed – which of course they knew and would sometimes flaunt before me. Then, as if to demonstrate just how juvenile I really was, I would disgrace myself by bursting into tears.

One night, after just such an upset – I have no idea how it came about – my mother took me on her lap and tried to console me by showing me an all but invisible scar in the middle of her forehead. She actually guided my index finger to it with her hand, which enabled me to make it out in the naked space between her eyebrows. I could even feel it; or thought I could. More like a tiny star than a line, it was the mark of an accident that had happened to her perhaps thirty years before, in Varniai. She had been about ten years old then. She and a friend of hers, she told me, were playing a game outside the house. Mary, the sister nearest to her in age, wanted to join in the game, but my mother and her friend were determined to keep her out of it.

Menuchah heard the children arguing and came outside to tell the two older ones to let Mary into the game. But they wouldn't hear of it. Eventually they decided there was only one way to get rid of her. They ran off down the road, knowing that Mary would be unable to catch up with them. My mother no longer remembered where they intended to hide. They did not reach their destination, anyway. Running at full speed, she tripped and fell.

Having reached that stage in telling the story, at least three decades after the event, she again lifted my index finger to her forehead. The tip of my finger covered completely the indentation at which she was pointing: a tiny pale star, still shining on her large brow, which I had never seen before and would always see thereafter.

She had fallen on a sharp stone, embedded point upward in the road. She had also scraped her knees and the palms of her hands. But it was the blow on the forehead that counted. Dizzy and bleeding, she staggered back to the house. Menuchah washed the wound and put a bandage around her head.

'But I could see she was cross with me,' my mother said. 'She felt it was my own fault. And so did I, really. It was like a punishment – because I hadn't listened to her, and because we'd been unkind to Mary. I was sure father would be cross with me too, but he was very nice about it. He said we'd been silly girls to run away, and Mary had been just as silly to bother us, when we didn't want to play with her. She should have left us alone.'

My mother fell silent and I thought the story was over. Then she added in a dreamy, almost luxurious fashion, 'I had to stay in bed for a couple of days because of it.'

Now that I have retold the story, I find myself wondering whether Heshel Melamed ever had occasion to recall the incident. All the elements I recognized in it – my mother's friendship with someone outside the family; the game she and her friend were playing; Mary's importunities; the older ones' dash to freedom; its painful and humiliating end; her mother's coldness; his kindness – all of these were as vivid to me as everything else that made the story seem so remote and hard to imagine. My mother ten years old? My mother playing a game outside? *Running?* And all this in Varniai, in Lithuania, on the other side of the world, where no one I knew had ever gone but whence so many of them had come – that bleak, sombre territory where people spoke only Yiddish and Russian to one another (or so I thought, not even knowing then that there was such a language as Lithuanian, since no one had ever mentioned it to me); where they paid for their purchases in roubles and copecks; where snow fell from the sky (I had never seen snow); where there were alien, threatening people called 'peasants' who lived in mysterious, Red Riding Hood 'woods' and 'villages' (in South Africa we had straggling, sandy *dorps*, but it was clear to me that a *dorp* was not a village); and where there were small towns like Varniai as well as big cities in which Jews like ourselves were not a thin sprinkling among incomparably larger numbers of gentiles, but in some places made up as much as half the population.

There too was the grandfather I would never see, whom I had always known as an inhabitant of a kingdom even more mysterious and distant than Lithuania, the region where the dead were taken when they had finally ceased to be. But there he was in the midst of it all, being kind to my injured, penitent mother. Kinder to her than her mother had been. As kind to me, in his way, as she was, telling this tale in order to comfort me and to point out an obscure moral.

For various reasons I suspect that my large-browed, soft-haired, double-chinned mother, Liebe, was her father's favourite among his children. This naturally makes me think well of him, since she was my favourite too, despite the quasi-sexual glamour that her much younger sisters in Johannesburg had for me as a small boy. (Not so quasi, actually.) It was Liebe, not any of the other girls, whom he allowed to receive private lessons in German and Russian, in spite of his disapproval of his wife's reading habits and the books he knew his daughter would be encouraged to read. More remarkably still, given his hostility to the Zionist movement, he arranged for Liebe also to receive lessons in modern, spoken Hebrew: a version of the language which was then in its infancy. She was a diligent pupil of it too. When she visited Israel for the first and only time in her late fifties, some of the locals congratulated her on the 'purity' of her Hebrew. But her own entirely secular hostility to the Zionist idea and the Zionist achievement was so strong she used the language in speaking to them only when she was forced to do so.

Long after the episode with Mary which I have just described, her father also allowed her to appear on the stage at a public function in the town – a concert or a reception for a visiting dignitary of some kind. From the platform she recited poems in Yiddish and Hebrew. 'Wearing *powder*!' one of her sisters told me at least fifty years later, still astonished that he should have given such latitude to her. 'Our Liebe! In front of everybody!' And he raised no objection when, quite off her own bat, she went to Mr Klovnetzky, the owner of the biggest shop in Varniai, and got a position in it as his cashier. No doubt her wages were a welcome supplement to the family income.

This was at the beginning of 1914. Six months later the Germans invaded Russia. The family fled eastwards.

It was not my mother but my aunt Sadie who told me about their flight from the approaching German army. The entire Jewish community of Varniai, she said, was involved in it. Most people went on foot, carrying whatever possessions they could. Somehow a small wagon, drawn by a single horse, was procured for the family, along with a Lithuanian driver. (I now know exactly what kind of wagon it was, having recently seen so many on the country roads of Lithuania: it had a high seat for two in front, upright ends at its back and front, and a body like a long barrow or oversized coffin, with inward-sloping sides.) Menuchah, who was – inevitably – nursing her most recent child, rode on it, along with the smaller children; Heshel Melamed and the others took turns walking and riding alternately. The furniture was left in the locked-up house.

I did not hear from Sadie about this sudden flight until long after my mother's death; since the story was new to me I could not help wondering if she was not misremembering or exaggerating the event. Yet she was adamant about it, both in speaking to me and later when she wrote about it in a letter; and sure enough, in the Schoenburgs' book, from which I have already quoted a couple of times, a single, stark, confirmatory sentence appears in the entry on Varniai: 'During World War I the Jews left.'

The authors do not say why they went. Nor did Sadie. In the Second World War almost every Jew capable of fleeing from the advancing Germans tried to do so; they all knew that the approaching army, as if carrying some terrible plague, was bringing with it a degree of organized hatred unprecedented even in the history of anti-Semitism. (Though no one then had a notion of the demented lengths to which they planned to carry it; no one knew that immediately behind the front-line regiments were special units, the *Einsatzkommandos*, which had already undergone training in the techniques of mass murder.) In 1914, by contrast, the Jews of eastern Europe looked on Germany as a country of high cultural and economic achievement; many of the more ambitious among them aspired to go there in order to acquire the education in science, medicine and engineering denied to them in Poland and Russia.

Paradoxically, that was why they were compelled to flee. The Jewish admiration for things German was of course known to the Tsarist government. At the outbreak of the war, therefore, the order came from Moscow that the Jews in the most westerly provinces of the empire were to be evacuated eastwards immediately. To quote another historian of the community:

Since the Jews of the western districts, like all their brethren in the Russian empire, had been treated for over a century as enemies of the state, the government would not credit them with any sentiment of loyalty . . . and since they spoke a language of German origin [i.e. Yiddish], it was thought but natural that they would fraternize with the invaders and help them. Hence, soon after the outbreak of hostilities, the commander-in-chief, Grand Duke Nicolaievitch, ordered the evacuation at short notice of the entire Jewish population of those districts.

Also, in a few districts, Kaunas and Siauliai among them, gangs of peasants and townsfolk had seized on the disorder of the times and the approach of the German armies to launch pogroms against their local Jewish communities.

From such outbreaks of banditry Varniai had been spared. Nevertheless every family in the community, the rabbi's among them, had to pack up its portables, shut its house and set out along the summer-dusty roads leading to the east. The journey was a hard one for all compelled to make it. But Heshel Melamed had reasons of his own for finding it especially difficult. To him, every totter and sway of the ramshackle wagon must have felt like yet another reproachful shake given to his conviction that Lithuania was the best of all countries for a pious Jew. Had he taken his wife and children to America they would have been forced to leave their home – but not in this fashion; they would have had to go on a long journey – but not to so uncertain a destination. Seeing his own fear in his children's faces, hearing them complaining of the thirst and hunger he too was suffering from, no doubt he shouted angrily at them, as any father would; and then attempted to comfort and reassure them. A faintness which was also a darkness mounted in his head and sank down again. Something was wrong with him; something that was not just the consequence of fatigue and anxiety. He said so to his wife. Menuchah told him to stay with her on the wagon; he should not feel obliged so often to join the older children walking alongside. Sadie could remember hearing the exchanges between them. I imagine the flat countryside intermittently withdrawing from him, going elsewhere, vanishing from his sight. Then it would silently reassemble itself: there was a copse, a field, a cottage, some ruts in the road. A bird. A stream. In rote fashion, and yet with the utmost sincerity, he muttered the prayers that came to his lips.

It never occurred to him that his flight before that approaching army might one day be seen as a dress rehearsal for what was to take place twenty-five years later. For all of us the future is a land we can delineate only in terms of what is already known to us – which is not how it will ever be. So it is my problem, not his, that when I think of him on that cart, or walking with his children alongside it, my mother among them, I cannot get out of my mind what was to happen a generation later in Kelme and Varniai and countless places like them, when an entire people tried to flee and found their murderers waiting for them wherever they turned.

After two days and a night on the road, the family arrived in Kelme, where his in-laws, the Oppenheims, lived. That is as far as they went – a mere twenty-five miles east of Varniai. I have no idea how much further all the other fugitives from the town travelled and where they took shelter. My suspicion is that the thirty-six or forty-eight hours the family had been on the road were sufficient for the Grand Duke's authority to have become radically eroded, in the country districts at least. But perhaps the rabbi's family, with the help of their hosts in Kelme, managed to secure a special exemption for themselves.

Room was made for the new arrivals in the house of Menuchah's parents. Heshel Melamed spent a few days in bed,
recovering from the journey. His father-in-law, Rabbi Zvi Yakov,
was himself bedridden too, which could not have made things
easy for anyone. Some years before her death my aunt Sadie
wrote down for me her recollections of their arrival: 'By then
Zvi Yakov was old, senile, and very frail. In the *shtetl* he was
still regarded as a *gaon*, however – a great rabbi . . . I remember
him vividly; he had very blue eyes and delicate features.' A
short while afterwards the Germans came. They behaved 'like
gentlemen' throughout, according to my mother. She saw a fair
amount of them during the period that the family remained in
Kelme, since her knowledge of German and Russian enabled
her to work as an intermediary between the occupiers, the
Jewish community and other groups in the town. Apparently
no stigma was attached to this activity.

Then the family returned to Varniai, no doubt to the relief
of the in-laws they were leaving behind. They found the house
as they had left it many weeks before. Annele, the maid, whom
Heshel Melamed had never liked, had gone back to her village
when the house was closed and did not return. ('It took a whole
world war,' he said sardonically to one of his daughters, 'to get
rid of Annele.') After a delay arising from the unsettledness of
the times, his oldest son, Leib, was sent to a *yeshiva* in Telz.
My mother began working again in Klovnetzky's store. Notwithstanding wartime shortages, some of them severe enough
to result in spells of outright hunger, everything went on pretty
much as it always had, except that the authorities ruling over
the district were German now, not Russian.

As between these two species of overlord, my mother pre-
ferred the Germans. They were always polite and orderly, she
said. Now that she was home again, however, her father forbade
her to speak to any members of the occupying army. It would
not have been seemly. Nevertheless, she did sometimes manage

to have conversations in the shop or elsewhere with some of the officers.

Romances?

'Oh, don't be silly.'

Occasionally guarded convoys of Russian prisoners passed through, on foot, stumbling westwards. They 'looked bad', my mother said.

How – bad?

'Hungry . . . Also – their feet . . .' She gestured unhappily downwards, towards her own small, neatly shod feet. 'They would wrap them in anything they could find. Rags. Straw.'

[5]

Let me jump ahead for a moment, in order to explain the document below.

My mother arrived in South Africa in 1920. She enrolled immediately in a night school in Johannesburg; her ambition was to take her matriculation and then to try to study for a degree at the university there. At the end of the year she did matriculate and was awarded a bursary to cover her university fees. However, she attended courses for only a term or two before marrying my father and going to live with him on a remote railway siding in the Orange Free State.

I still have a few possessions from her early years. Among them are three or four exercise books she filled while taking her lessons in the night school. Here, transcribed from one of these books, is an essay she wrote for her English teacher. It appears between two other compositions entitled, with a kind of fatal recognizability, 'A Character Sketch of Shakespeare's Henry the Fifth' and 'The Value of Foreign Languages'. Though her writing is often ungrammatical and unidiomatic, the essay seems to me quite an impressive piece of work, considering that she had arrived in the country just a few months before and, as far as I know, had not studied English before leaving Lithuania. The vivid, tender description of her father after the rigours of the Yom Kippur fast is probably the most expressive detail in the passage; its sense of foreboding is made all the stronger by the fact that she does not name the 'seriously ill' member of the family she later speaks of, and leaves deliberately unresolved the hope that the 'worst' might not happen to him. (When she wrote it, she knew that it had.) As for the saintly Mr N.L., to whose virtues most of the essay is devoted, I know nothing about him other than what is said here.

Reminiscences

I was sitting and thinking and a peculiar feeling overwhelmed me. Somehow the present vanished. And I was carried far, far away.

Shadows of men and women rose before my mental eye, filled the spaces. They all looked in such a friendly manner at me and smiled.

And from among all of the faces that were long ago near and dear to me one face especially attracted my attention.

Gradually my memory established the man whose face I recalled. He was an old friend of our house that used to come to see us, not paying the least attention to the weather, whether it was raining or stormy. This man with his slender figure, his vigorous movements, and good eyes, is weaved into the days of my past and I cannot think of them without remembering him.

Other pictures arise and among them one that used to repeat itself regularly every year late in the evening after the Day of Atonement. My father, having something in his expression that reminded us of the just-elapsed fast, was yet full of anticipation of a happy year. And it made for something remarkably touching in his face, this nuance of light and shadow, the weariness and earnestness of the day mingled with the hopes of the evening. And during that evening our friend used to appear to inquire if we were not too much weakened by the day of fasting. A special attention he paid then to the smaller ones, to whom fasting was a novelty that strained and delighted them at the same time. And his appearing then used to accentuate the confidence that all the hopes we cherished will come true in the future.

I remember distinctly a night of another kind. It was a late and obscure autumn night. It rained a showery cold rain and outside was anything but friendly. And in the house? Also from there the cosiness had vanished. One felt the strained mood that characterizes a house, where a member of the family is seriously ill. All of a sudden, a knock at the door. We at once understood who could call in this weather. It was he, our friend, our faithful N.L. And something like a relief came over us. It seemed that he brought with him all the power of his faith that God will help. I went with him to call the doctor.

Night looked very dark and severe. But it was he who for the moment had banished my fears. Perhaps the worst would not happen.

He was poor and could help materially but little, but he brought a gift that is occasionally more precious than anything else – he brought to his friends his deepest sympathy in their sorrow; his sincere attachment to the distressed and the lonely ones.

With its description of a household stricken first by illness and fear, later by sorrow, distress and loneliness, the essay manages to suggest the extent to which Heshel Melamed's last few years were dominated for himself and his family by an often repudiated, ever-returning awareness that something treacherous and implacable was at work within him; and that no medicine, no enforced periods of rest, no distractions, no prayers, were likely to turn it aside. Nor was it to be assuaged by the pretence that nothing was amiss, that he and others were simply mistaken, and that in another month or year he would be free of the symptoms troubling him and the whole episode would have receded into the past, as his childhood had – or even his first marriage.

However, it was not only his illness that he had to contend with at this time. His life (what was left of it) was also oppressed by anxiety about his oldest son, Leib, and by a deeper disappointment with his second son, Michael. Family tradition demanded that both youngsters go to a *yeshiva*, to study for the rabbinate; it suggested also that their place of study should be Telz, a town about thirty miles north of Varniai, where their grandfather, Zvi Yakov Oppenheim, himself by now also close to death, and their great-grandfather, Michael Yitzhak Oppenheim, had each acquired his 'certification' as a rabbi.

So off the two of them went: Leib first, naturally. When he came back for his holidays he did not hide from his parents how unhappy he was in Telz. He disliked the school, the teachers and the other students; though he was a boy of intellectual inclinations, he positively hated what he was supposed to be studying (the Bible, the tractates of the Talmud and the accretions of commentaries on both), and the ostensible reason why he was studying it (so that he too could in due course become a rabbi). Sixty years later, living in rural surroundings in Warwickshire, England, and a profoundly unhappy man still, he was to write a brief memoir in which he described his time in the *yeshiva* with a scorn and bitterness which the passing of time had done nothing to moderate. Everything in it and about it seemed equally contemptible to him: the squalor of the students' living conditions; the tedium of the texts put before them, from which no escape was offered into other forms of learning; the futile, repetitive, casuistical discussions of those texts in which everyone was expected to take part; the obedience he was expected to display towards teachers he had no regard for and a system of thought and belief that, in his view, had long outlived itself.

At home he wept (a grown boy!) over the waste of his life. He spoke of never going back; of running away from home; even of committing suicide. His father tried to encourage him by speaking of God's will, of the dignity of a rabbi's position in the community, of the examples offered him by his distinguished forebears, of the pleasures of a life devoted to study and prayer. Fortunately, the rabbi did not know (nor did I, until I read Leib's memoir) that the only episode from his days in the *yeshiva* which he would later recall with any pleasure was a 'homosexual experience' with another boy – which, he wrote, without giving any details, 'excited him greatly'.

Still, he went back. He put up with it, after a fashion. There was nowhere else for him to go; until he reached his majority there was nothing else he could do. Or so he felt. Compared with his younger brother, Leib was ultimately docile enough. Michael, the younger brother in question, gave his father grief of a related yet different kind. He too was dispatched to Telz in due course, though not to the establishment Leib was attending. But Michael stayed in his *yeshiva* for a few weeks only. Then, without even telling his older brother in the neighbouring institution what he was about to do, he set off to walk home. Footsore, dirty, hungry – a quavering, obstinate stripling, proud of what he had done and overcome by the enormity of it – he told his father that he was never going back.

Leib had said the same thing several times. But Michael's manner in making this declaration was different. His face was tearless; his voice was without expression, as if he was talking of a decision taken by someone else, not himself.

Another disappointment! Another blow in the face! One that Heshel Melamed felt all the more painfully for a reason he could not admit to himself or to any other member of the family, except perhaps his wife. (Though my mother was old and acute enough to know why he felt a particular grief over Michael's defection.) Leib may have carried the burden of being the oldest son, the one who, it was simply assumed, would follow the example of the generations before him. But on Michael, excitable, skinny little Michael, their father had pinned greater hopes yet. Leib was the 'kindly' son; everyone said what a gentle, good-hearted young man he was. Of course Heshel Melamed valued these qualities in him. Michael's gifts, however, he valued more. Michael was the cleverer of the two. He had always been quicker at his books, more articulate in argument, more agile-minded. Some people had rashly spoken of him as a *wunderkind* in the making. He had the potential, his father had long been convinced, to become a truly famous rabbi, a man whose name would be carried far beyond the circle of provincial somebodies and nobodies among whom he, Heshel Melamed, had always lived. Then he would share in the lustre of his son's achievements. Then even his wife's family would be forced to acknowledge how indebted they were to him.

Instead of which . . .

He took to his bed, as he was often compelled to do anyway, and remained there for many days. Menuchah interceded on Michael's behalf. He was only a boy; he should be forgiven; kindness would do more to bring him around than anger. Hearing her pleas, her husband could not help feeling (and saying) that he was the one who was entitled to consideration and compassion from Michael; not the other way around. The boy was deliberately betraying his own gifts; he was also betraying his father just when everyone knew him to be 'failing'. The last thing he needed was this kind of vexation. The doctor, by this time a frequent visitor to the house, said so too. The younger children (five girls and a boy) were constantly being hushed, told to tread more softly about the house, even sent away to other families in the town. Michael himself remained half in hiding, keeping out of his father's way as much as possible. This state of affairs went on for several weeks. As a result of his wife's intercessions it was finally agreed that Michael should go to study in Siauliai, a town with which, like Telz, the Oppenheim family had long had a connection.

Off he went. A month later he did it all again. The whole business. Got up one morning and stole away. Turned up, famished and exhausted, at the door.

It was at this time that the rabbi's youngest daughter, Reevee, and the only one of his children still surviving as I write these words, acquired the solitary, fragmentary memory she has of him.

This is what she remembers. Her father came into the house. It must have been during one of the winter months, for he was wearing a long, black, fur coat. She ran to meet him and clasped him around the knees. That was as far as she could reach. She pressed her face into his coat. She could see nothing but the darkness of the fur; feel nothing but its softness against her cheeks.

That is all. She was then not yet four years old. She told me this anecdote in her eighty-second year. We were in a private room in the Royal Overseas League, St James's, London, where she had arranged a dinner party for those of her nephews, nieces and their spouses who were living in England. She had made the trip from the United States for this one occasion. Her body was thin and erect; her voice clear; her expression animated; her hair beautifully groomed. She wore an elegant, formal, high-collared blouse. An expensive ring glittered on a single finger of each slender hand. As she spoke her mouth puckered forward with pleasure and recollective excitement. Her eyes – darker than my mother's; as dark as Heshel Mela-med's – shone like a girl's.

A few months after Reevee hugged him around the knees (and shortly before the death of his aged father-in-law in Kelme), he finally succumbed. His body was carried up the mild slope to the tree-shaded cemetery on the outskirts of Varniai, where it still lies.

The 'worst' that my mother feared had taken place. That it was also the 'best' for her and for all of them remained hidden in the unformed, unknowable future. The widow and children were left husbandless, fatherless, houseless, incomeless. At the time of his death the children ranged in age from my mother, who was twenty-one, to Reevee, who was turning four. The grief felt by Menuchah and the older children was inextricable from their fear of the future and the shame of knowing themselves to be dependent on others. The little ones knew only that everything had changed, and for the worse.

Poverty and homelessness were not all they had to fear. Between 1915, when the German armies entered the country, and 1921, when the independent republic of Lithuania was admitted to the League of Nations, the authorities claiming sovereignty over the territory, or over different parts of it, changed about a dozen times. The ending of the Russo-German war in 1918 produced even greater dangers and instabilities than those the population had already been through. Disorganized German, Bolshevik, White Russian, Polish and Lithuanian armies advanced and retreated in random-seeming fashion; bandit groups owing no loyalty to any state or political movement, and notorious for their ferocity (towards the Jews especially), fought each other and everyone else. From various corners of the country came reports or rumours of starvation, outbreaks of cholera and typhus, the sacking of this town or that. More than once the bereaved family in Varniai fled into the woods nearby, along with everybody else from the town, and remained cowering there overnight or longer. Sometimes they heard firing and shouting; at other times nothing at all. If everything remained silent for long enough, they emerged and crept back to their homes, hoping to find them intact.

All this, and how much these flights to the woods had frightened her, were also among my aunt Reevee's earliest memories.

Eventually one part of the family returned to Kelme (my mother among them); others went to stay with cousins in Siauliai. Something had to be done. The relations in Kelme were desperate to get rid of the burden that had been placed on them. At the opposite end of the world, in South Africa, were many kinsmen on both Menuchah's side and her late husband's:

for reasons I will explain shortly, many more of them had migrated to that remote country than to the United States.

So letters went back and forth between Johannesburg and Kelme. Amazingly enough, the wars and political upheavals in Lithuania and the countries around it did not put a stop to this correspondence. Nor did the fact that it took a full six weeks for a letter to travel in each direction. In a manner characteristic of the people involved, and of the period, the relations in South Africa duly made money available for the family's passage out, on the understanding that the sums would be repaid once the newcomers were settled and the older children – my mother, Leib and Michael – had begun to earn a living. The family in Kelme also advanced a small sum. Whatever remained from the house in Varniai was disposed of.

Documents left by my mother speak almost as clearly as she ever did about the unrest that gripped the country during her father's last years and in the months preceding the family's departure for South Africa. Here, for instance, is the beige-coloured post-office savings book she had used in the days of Russian rule, complete with two-headed imperial eagle on its cover, as well as an imposing title in Cyrillic lettering: POTCHTOVO-TELEGRAPHIYA: GOSIDARSTVENYA: SVEREGA-TEPUNYAIKASSA. The last withdrawal from it was made late in 1915; it shows a sad little balance of 2.25 roubles, which remains to her credit to this day. Her passport, by contrast, uses the Lithuanian and German languages only. A tall, four-sided document printed on cheap paper and devoid of a cover of any kind, it is dated September 1920 and is issued in Kaunas by the newly established 'Respublika Lietuvos'. It gives her occupation as 'student' (*Lehrerin*) and her usual place of abode (*Ständiger Wohnort*) as Varniai (spelt Worny) – though by then the dispersed family was no longer living there.

Inside the document are visas issued by, among others, a

M. Reboul, the Colonel-Commandant of the French Military Mission in Lithuania, who mysteriously takes it on himself to authorize her travel across the Polish Corridor (*au travers le couloir Polonais*) to Danzig. His Britannic Majesty's Lieutenant-Colonel Wholly Illegible, on the other hand, insists on giving his formal address as Vilna/Vilnius, but the stamp on the passport shows that he actually issued the visa to her in Kovno/Kaunas, since Vilna/Vilnius was then under siege by the Polish army. (Both versions of both names are carefully given each time, as if diplomatic offence might be caused by omitting one or the other.) This visa – 'good for the single journey to South Africa through the United Kingdom' – cost my mother ten shillings. The equally obliging consuls of defeated Germany and neutral Netherlands have no military titles to sport – a fact of some political significance in itself, no doubt. Of yet another visa I can make no sense at all; it seems to have been issued by a country called Skyrius, which I cannot believe ever existed. Not even there. Not even then. Perhaps it was nothing more than her exit visa from Lithuania.

Similar passports, bearing identical visas, were presumably issued to Leib and Michael, and to their mother, whose passport would have covered the remaining children (Mary, Rae, Max, Sadie, Zippy and Reevee). The entire party travelled together.

Like Heshel Melamed, they too had a formal photograph of themselves taken before they went abroad. It is the only pre-migration picture of them to have survived.

The widow Menuchah, who in a year has lost both her father and her husband, sits at a small table; her hand rests on an outsize book – a prop provided for artistic reasons, I assume, by the photographer. Her face, tilted upwards, has a curiously naked, unadorned look. I suspect that it has this appearance to me because she was so much more wrinkled when I knew her than she is here. Reevee, the youngest child, is old enough to sit by herself, but is confined to a chair equipped with elaborate arms, no doubt to discourage her from toppling out of it. On the floor is a carpet so threadbare that the lines of the coarse floorboards can be seen through it, as well as all around it.

To my eye the nine children look extraordinarily, even parodically, Russian in an old-fashioned, 'enlightened', Chekhovian manner. They could have come straight from an elaborately assembled play in London's West End. The bobbed hair of the girls, the wide sailor's collar Sadie is wearing, the bushy, artistic tie hanging from Mary's neck, the cloth flower stitched just above the hem of Zippy's dress, Max's student jacket, complete with tiny stand-up collar and brass buttons – all contribute to the impression. No one smiles. Leib and Michael are beardless and hatless – sans all orthodox Jewish appendages – thus demonstrating that they have already cast aside the rules their father had lived by. Befitting their newly acquired status as the men of the family, they are seated on each side of their mother. Poor Max's head is completely shaven, because that was what used to be done to people suffering from ringworm.

Already they are out of their father's reach. Soon, any moment now, they will be on their way to distant, improbable South Africa. The dead man's glasses, notebook, studio portrait and a few other items are packed in Menuchah's bags. He will remain in Varniai, secure in the only place where the Nazis will never be able to get hold of him.

Here is another essay I have copied from one of the exercise books used by my mother at her night school in Johannesburg. This essay, written in preparation for her German examination, is entitled *Meine Eindrücken bei der Durchreise durch Deutschland*.* The translation is mine.

* 'My Impressions of a Journey Through Germany'.

The afternoon was growing colder when we reached the German border. It was getting dark. We were full of the impressions of the day. Sad indeed were our thoughts. We had left our country of birth and the people we loved there, our friends and acquaintances. An inexpressible love for whatever one has always had before one's eyes is always preserved by our nature and placed deep in the heart.

The whole day the sky had been clear and the air had been warm. It was one of those days in early spring which is like a freely bestowed gift from the ample summer ahead. A refreshing scent rose from the fields. At the border we left the train and our bags were cursorily [*flächlich*] inspected. Everyone around us was speaking German. We saw German faces and uniforms. Unwillingly we remembered the war, the occupation, the frightening times, the violent events. The least commotion reminded us of all this. But the formalities were soon completed and we could go on.

By the time we got to Königsberg the carriage was very full. Some people were standing. One could detect the nervous excitement that grips people when they are embarked on a long journey. After some time I too took the opportunity to speak in German. It was late at night when we arrived in Königsberg. The main railway station and the many waiting trains made a great impression on us provincials. So did the busyness of everything around the station. We had to get out of the train and spend the night there. The big surprise at the hotel was the calm welcome given us and the friendliness of the people.

On the second day we continued our journey to Berlin. In order to avoid the Polish Corridor we had to go by ship from Pilau to Schweinemunde. The crossing was very rough and some of us suffered greatly from seasickness. It was an experience that shattered one's pride. We had only a single day in Berlin, to look at the monuments and some of the huge shops like Tietz and Wertheim. At first glance Berlin gave an impression of unbounded appetite and luxury.

Soon we were on our way again. The friendly landscapes and the sunshine helped to raise our mood, and with hearts full of cheerful expectations for the future we awaited our arrival at the Netherlands border.

The reference in that essay to their having to 'avoid the Polish Corridor' shows that the assurance of M. Reboul, the head of the French mission in Kaunas, had not been sufficient to make the family feel that it would be safe for them to travel through '*le couloir Polonais*'. No doubt this was because newly independent Poland and newly independent Lithuania were then still at war with one another. Stamps on my mother's passport show that the family crossed the border between Germany and Holland at Oldenzaal, on 19 October 1920, and arrived in Harwich, England, on the following day. The next stamp reads 'Table Bay, Cape Town', exactly a month later.

Not surprisingly there is another essay in her English book which describes the arrival in the new country.*

On the eve of the arrival in Cape Town I was told to be on the deck early in the morning, before sunrise, since the scenery of Cape Town and the mountains is very beautiful from the sea. I awoke and hurried to the deck; our steamer stood still, as if it was resting from its last convulsions. Here and there I saw passengers coming from their cabins. I looked around and saw a mountain before me with tiny houses and fires at its foot. The sun was not yet rising and yet the mountain looked purple. The sea was quiet and grey. Little time could be spared for contemplation. The reality reminded itself to us energetically.

I think the newcomer is very agreeably surprised with Cape Town. First, the novelty of being again on dry land, and then the warmth and sunshine that can be enjoyed so fully. We spent there very little time, but the impression Cape Town has left is a favourable one. The

---

*My mother was (quite fairly) awarded a 'D' for English in her matriculation examination, as against a 'B' for German.

mountains and the sea give such a wonderful frame for this quiet town.

The long train journey from the Cape to Transvaal can be called adventurous for immigrants, who do not understand a word of the language that is spoken around them, and for whom, to ask for a cup of tea is like an adventure.

Then the first day in Johannesburg. The deserts the day before; and the splendid European town the day after. I think the South African immigrant is very often struck with these contrasts. Only a country where the white settlement is little more than a hundred years old can boast of these contrasts. The half-naked kaffir and most fashionably dressed up lady give us good examples of them. Phenomena that we come across every day in Johannesburg make us think of the great distance that the progress of mankind has crossed. If it has led to a greater degree of perfection, to happiness, to fulfilling the longings which have brought people from all ends of the world here – that is another question.

PART TWO

South Africa

[6]

The Jewish community in Lithuania amounted to less than 5 per cent of the total Jewish population in the 'Pale of Settlement', the areas of the Tsarist empire where Jews were allowed to live. Between 1880 and 1914, when Jews streamed out of the Pale in numbers unparalleled before or after, substantial numbers of the migrants from Lithuania made their way to Cape Town. For them, South Africa came second only to the United States as a chosen destination. Figures gathered by the British colonial authorities in Cape Town show that even the outbreak of the Anglo-Boer War at the turn of the century did not greatly discourage them from heading in that direction. In the period from 1895 to 1914 alone some 40,000 'Russian' immigrants, all of whom were in fact Jews, entered the country. A small minority of them came from other parts of the empire, from Latvia and White Russia mainly; the rest from Lithuania. My own guess – and it is no more than a guess – is that as many as one in five of the Jews who left Lithuania during this period went to South Africa.

If only more of them had seized the opportunity they had then! Not long after the end of the First World War South Africa's borders were effectively closed to immigrants from eastern Europe. So were those of the United States and most other countries. The next twenty years saw a total of only about 5,000 Jews from Lithuania arriving at the Cape.

A petty number, agreed. A catastrophically small one, in view of what was soon to happen. But that inter-war figure meant that as many Jews from Lithuania found shelter in South Africa during those years as in any other country in the world. Palestine and the mighty United States included.

Heshel Melamed's widow and nine children were of course among the lucky ones. *Malgré lui.*

The discovery of gold on the Witwatersrand (1882) coincided almost exactly with the start of mass emigration of Jews from the Russian empire to the west. But to make so many Jews from that one particular corner of the empire choose South Africa as their destination required a further coincidence. Circumstances duly provided it. It went by the improbably humble name of Sammy Marks.

He is remembered in South Africa today chiefly because his house – a huge, iron-roofed, colonial-style, no-expense-spared mansion built in the veld between Johannesburg and Pretoria – has been turned into a popular tourist attraction. Originally he came from an insignificant place called Neustadt-Sugint, in the Suvalkai district of Lithuania, near the border of east Prussia. ('His parents were simple, God-fearing people, his father eking out a living as an itinerant tailor among the Lithuanian peasants.') From Neustadt-Sugint he went to England; from England to South Africa. After a couple of years in Cape Town he set out to try his luck on the recently opened diamond fields in Kimberley, where a number of German and English Jews were rapidly acquiring great wealth and fame. He did not manage to emulate them. Nor did he ever succeed in becoming one of the major gold-mining magnates ('Randlords') on the Witwatersrand. He made his fortune in less 'glamorous' enterprises: in the coal fields of the eastern

Transvaal and northern Natal; in brick fields, breweries, distilleries, sugar refineries; in farming with new varieties of maize, cattle and potatoes; and in a host of similar undertakings. He was in fact South Africa's first true industrial entrepreneur (thus setting an example that was to be followed in more modest fashion by many of the Litvaks who arrived later); he was also the only 'Uitlander' to became a trusted counsellor to Paul Kruger, the last President of the Boer republic of the Transvaal.

But his rise to financial and political eminence in the new country did not make him forget the folks back home. Still less did they forget him. Unlike the Jewish 'Randlords' from Germany and England – Barnatos, Joels, Beits, Philipses and so forth – Sammy Marks was one of their own, after all. 'His success . . . had a notable effect,' write the historians of the community I have just quoted.

It is he who is regarded as the chief pioneer of Lithuanian Jewish migration to South Africa . . . It is almost impossible to imagine today the sensation created throughout Lithuania when in 1892 Samuel Marks sent the munificent sum of £1,000 to Neustadt-Sugint for the restoration of its synagogue.

A much smaller contribution to this migration was also made by a member of my mother's family. A cousin on the Oppenheim side, Meyer Dovid Hersch by name, arrived in the country some time before Sammy Marks. He was no magnate or industrialist; merely a journalist, from the little town of Yanishok originally, who took it on himself to let the people back home know of the claims of this distant, unstable, yet curiously enticing outpost of the British empire. His articles appeared in journals published in St Petersburg and Warsaw and were read with special attention all over Lithuania. He too was one of their own, which meant a great deal to those particular readers. While his reports did not try to hide the difficulties the immigrants would encounter in South Africa, overall they presented a strongly favourable picture of it. He himself eventually went back to Lithuania and (so far as I know) remained there; but by then his work had had its effect on the plans and ambitions of many of his fellow countrymen.

His own family among them, of course. The result was that by the time the widowed Menuchah and her offspring arrived in South Africa, an extensive cousinhood was already settled there. Hersches, Horwitzes, Austokers, Levys, Segals – kinsmen all, either on her side of the family or her husband's – they had spread themselves in every direction. Some of them had settled in Johannesburg, or in mining towns nearby on the Witwatersrand; others were to be found keeping hotels or stores on remote railway sidings like Paardeberg, or in sun-stricken *dorps* like Modder River or Fauresmith: places consisting then, and still consisting today, of not much more than handfuls of scattered habitations. Each store was suspended on the glistening thread of the railway line which brought to the immigrants the merchandise they sold over their counters and which took their children back to the nearest state boarding schools at the end of every holiday.

In Lithuania the Jews had spread themselves into every remote corner of the country. In South Africa they did the same. Only, the spaces around them here were incomparably wider, the sky was higher, the sun stronger, the people (blacks, Boers, English, fellow Jews) much more thinly scattered.

Another life.

The newly arrived, lately bereaved family crammed itself into a rented, single-storeyed bungalow in Johannesburg. This was in the suburb of Doornfontein, one of the areas of the city in which Jewish immigrants congregated. The younger girls went to the nearest government junior and senior schools. Soon they were speaking English among themselves; Yiddish they used only in conversation with their mother. The boys or young men,

Leib, Michael and Max, found whatever employment they could. Like their oldest sister, they too enrolled at night schools. Her contribution to the family budget came from the tiny sums she earned as a Hebrew teacher. Later Leib followed her example, both in offering Hebrew lessons and in enrolling at the University of the Witwatersrand. Unlike my mother, however, he eventually graduated with a BA degree in Psychology. (A Freudian in the making.) With or without his degree he had a hard time earning a living. The only one of the brothers who showed any aptitude for business was Michael; but he lacked a quality for which the others, in speaking of him, always chose to use the German word *Sitzfleisch*. Patience. Stoicism. Stolidity.

Looking at the pre-migration photograph of the entire family described in the previous chapter, or at the few surviving snapshots of some of its members taken soon after their arrival in Johannesburg, I cannot help thinking what a vivid, disparate group the nine children form. Inevitably another thought follows that one. How much I now know about them of which they had not an inkling in the months after their arrival! How many hard questions was time to ask of them all, before it relentlessly delivered its answers!

I am not going to follow them collectively or individually through their lives. Nevertheless, I cannot restrain myself from exercising over them the divine power of hindsight. I know, for instance, that none of these nine young, bewildered, hopeful newcomers ever rose to a position of importance in the country's commercial, professional or intellectual life. None of them looked for a career in politics. There were to be no criminals or drunkards among them. None (so far as I know) ever appeared as co-respondent in a divorce case; none ever fathered or mothered an illegitimate child. Having rejected the faith into which they were born, none of them adopted another. One of them, however, to the scorn of the others, did come out as a supporter and admirer of apartheid.

OK. All that settled, much remains: vicissitudes they would never have been able to imagine beforehand, or (in many cases) would later have wished to be spared. Nine young people. Nine immigrants. Nine opportunities for those who came after them to gaze into Shakespeare's 'seeds of time'; to gaze into them retrospectively, of course, for how else can it be done?

Very well then. Which one of the nine will die at a much earlier age than the other eight? Which one will become by far the wealthiest of them? Which one will marry at a much later age than the rest? How many will separate from their spouses in middle age? How many will try to do so and not succeed? How many will die childless? Who will produce more children than any of the others? The baby boy of which one will die as a result of septicaemia setting in after his circumcision? Which one will lose a baby girl from pneumonia? Who will go to live in central Africa, 2,000 miles to the north, and, decades later, move to Worcester, Mass.? Which one, on the other hand, will work for almost forty years at the same desk in the same branch in Johannesburg of one of the country's major financial institutions?

How many of them will die of heart disease? Of cancer? Of old age? Which one will spend his last three decades hopelessly addicted to amphetamines? Which one will quarrel with the rest, and with his wife and children too, and end his life by putting a bullet through his head? (Taking care beforehand to shoot his last and only friend, his German shepherd dog.) Whose husband will commit suicide by jumping off a high building? Whose husband will have a leg amputated after what turned out to be a false diagnosis of bone cancer?

Who will have a career as a stage actress and a broadcaster? Who will marry a German Jewish music-lover? And who a notoriously 'difficult' Afrikaner? Who, during the Second World War, will be cut off with two companions (one of them wounded) behind the German lines, and yet after days in the

North African desert manage to bring all three back to his unit? Which of them will spend a lifetime as a counter-hand in other people's shops? How many of them will commit adultery? Which one will develop severe asthma late in life? Which one will be driven to a nervous breakdown by the hostility of his stepchildren? Who will become the mayoress of a small town? Who will work for a year among concentration camp survivors in north Italy and Austria? Which one will become a moderately successful farmer and then a wholly unsuccessful inventor? Who among them will go to their graves with secrets forever inaccessible to my hindsight or anyone else's?

Take up the photograph again. Nine lives in waiting. Nine escapees from the rifles and machine guns of the German *Einsatzkommandos* and from their Lithuanian hirelings; from the burial pits and pyres that would have consumed their bodies in their natal land. Nine young people spared as a result of their father's early death to make the best or worst of the opportunities given to them and denied to those they had left behind.

I go back again and again to that thought. I have to do so. As much as anything else it is what provokes me to seek them out now, and their father lying in the Varniai cemetery. Or to feel myself sought out by them.

For them, safely landed in South Africa, the privilege of vicissitude: success, failure, appetite, disappointment, wreckage, growth, an individual exit from existence. For the others, for the family in Kelme, for neighbours and townsfolk in Varniai, for the entire nation they were born into – nothing. A single, common fate.

On one side of the ocean, life. On the other, death.

> If you can look into the seeds of time,
> And say which grain will grow and which will not.

One other thing that can be said about them all, now that they have arrived safely in South Africa, is that they unanimously proceeded to reject everything their father had believed in. Some of them did so vocally, vehemently; others did it quietly, by default. None showed an interest in keeping up the 'old ways' which Heshel Melamed had thought of as more precious than his own life. In later years my mother and Mary, the sister nearest to her in age, obliged their spouses by seeing to it that most of the festive meals of the Jewish calendar were served in their homes at the right times – Passover, the New Year, the breaking of the fast on Yom Kippur. Neither of them concealed their feeling that they regarded these celebrations as matters of form merely. When Sabbath candles were lit in their households, as they were from time to time, the action was performed in prayerless fashion. In our house, though not in Mary's, that particular chore was almost always left to the black domestics. So was the cooking and presentation of the meals. The servants actually took far greater pride in getting the dishes and procedures 'right' than my mother ever did.

And she and Mary, compared to their siblings, were the observant ones! As a child I did not realize how unusual it was for an entire family to detach itself so abruptly from the beliefs and practices of its forebears in general and its parents in particular. I took it for granted; that was simply how they behaved. Three things, I now realize, made their detachment from the ways of their own past, and the past of their people, all the more striking. The first was that it was not the consequence of a slow, guilty drift away from beliefs for which they retained a notional respect and from practices which they might have wished to continue, had doing so not demanded constant effort. On the contrary, their severance from the faith, and from almost all the forms through which it was expressed, was abrupt and thoroughgoing. (Most of their friends were Jewish, not surprisingly, but that was obviously a different matter.) Secondly, when it suited them they took pride in claiming descent from an unbroken line of rabbis, the Oppenheims, which could be traced at least as far back as the eighteenth century. The pride they took in their ancestry was, however, devoid of piety towards the faith which the ancestors themselves had maintained. Finally, their rejection of the Jewish God and all his demands did not lead them to adopt the banally left-wing views which attracted so many secular Jews of their generation. My aunts and uncles were inclined to go whoring after stranger gods: Freudianism in one case; an Anglophiliac snobbery in others; even (in another instance, and strangest of all) Afrikaner Nationalism.

The philosopher Hegel spoke about the 'cunning of reason'. What about the cunning of unreason? The compulsive re-creation and transmutation of the conflicts which each generation inherits from its predecessors? I have little doubt that Menuchah's belated access of piety sprang from a guilty conviction that Heshel Melamed's early death had been some kind of judgement on her; one which she could expiate only by spending the rest of her life in a display of obedience to him and to the God he had worshipped. His children, on the other hand, seized the opportunity given them by his death to align themselves definitively with their mother's earlier show of scepticism and to reject all that their father had stood for. Collectively they spurned what Leib, my uncle, the rabbi's oldest son and now in effect the family spokesman, referred to as 'the superstition and fetishism of the past'.

That was how he spoke of the faith of his ancestors. He would listen with a strong, guilty passion to gramophone records of eminent cantors intoning the Jewish liturgy; but it remained a matter of principle for him never to set foot in a synagogue, except for 'events' like weddings or funerals which it was impossible for him to avoid. Of the life that he himself had once led in the *shtetl* he spoke only with scorn and bitterness.

The truth is that the rabbi's children were infatuated by what they found on their arrival in South Africa: this more or less English-speaking outpost of the modern, developing, secularized West. They had a love affair not so much with South Africa itself as with the civilization of which it was a kind of rough-and-ready annexe. Danger, injustice and deprivation abounded in the new country they had come to; but so did hope, change, a sense of expectation unknown in the regions they had left behind.

So it had not been necessary for them to go to America in order to do exactly as their father had feared they would, given the chance. They found opportunity enough for it in provincial South Africa. For all the hardships they went through in the new country, and they went through many, they did not doubt that in leaving Lithuania they had exchanged night for the promise of day, superstition for the promise of reason, limitation and frustration for a hitherto unimaginable degree of personal autonomy.

Later, the terrible course of history proved even such terms inadequate to describe the fatefulness of the journey the family had undertaken. In leaving Lithuania for South Africa, they had exchanged an anonymous death at the hands of murderers for life itself.

Whereas their father had unwittingly chosen the former.

That was how his own children saw it. It would hardly occur to his grandchildren to do otherwise.

For the moment though, and for the last time, I want to leave all but one of the newcomers in that bungalow in Doornfontein, encased still in their ignorance of everything that lies ahead.

The exception I have chosen to make among them is my mother. Imagine that twelve years have passed since that morning outside Cape Town harbour, when she awoke and hurried to the deck of the steamer which had brought her there and saw a mountain 'with tiny houses and fires at its foot'.

In the intervening years she has become the mother of three boys, the youngest of whom has just turned four years old. (One other child has been lost in babyhood.) She has travelled overnight with the three boys from Johannesburg to Kimberley, where her husband – himself not greatly endowed with *Sitz-fleisch* – has just bought a bankrupt butter factory. Of Kimberley she knows nothing, other than that it is a place where diamonds are mined. Or, rather, a place where diamonds were once mined. It is common knowledge in South Africa at this time that Kimberley has sunk into an irreversible decline. Its mines are (wrongly) believed to be completely exhausted; its population has dwindled to a figure well below that of the smaller gold-mining centres like Germiston or Benoni, unknown outside South Africa, which are nothing more than Johannesburg's satellites. In Kimberley, she has been told, houses stand empty all over the town.

Yet this is where her husband has chosen to move. After the hardships of the depression years in Johannesburg, and the death of her fourth child, a baby daughter, she has no inclination to contest his decision.

She has still to learn of Kimberley's heat, its isolation, the drab flatness of its landscapes. She also has to learn, yet again, as she had during her relatively brief sojourn in the Orange Free State, how painfully she will miss her mother and siblings during the decades of quasi-exile from them that lie ahead.

Her husband has preceded her to Kimberley, in order to find accommodation for his family. Now he waits on the platform as the train pulls in. The older boys are greatly excited and start trying to pull pieces of luggage down from the racks overhead. My mother tries to calm them. In order to free her hands, she takes hold of her youngest son and passes him through the open window of the compartment into the arms of his father.

I was that son. I am that son still. I see my father smiling as he raises his hands to receive me.

It is early in March 1933. Just over two months previously, on 30 January, Hitler had become Chancellor of Germany.

[7]

So it is from there that my earliest memories are derived. The parched landscapes of Kimberley and the northern Cape gave me my deepest and most tenacious idea of what the world should look like; how its seasons should come and go; to what overweening heights its skies should rise. Houses should be brick-built, single-storeyed affairs, adorned with corrugated-iron roofs, wide *stoeps* and puny ornamental gables. Unless they were the huts lived in by blacks, in which case anything – mud, sacking, planks – would do. With big boulders on top, to keep the whole contraption from blowing away. Behind plate-glass windows and projecting canopies, shops too should huddle under iron roofs. Schools (our schools) should be imposing, multi-windowed affairs, ranged around quadrangles and segregated from the nearest roads by rugby fields, tennis courts and bike sheds in long rows. The rare schools for blacks, in their distant 'locations' or 'townships', should be about the height and size of those same bike sheds. All this, interspersed with open mines and mine dumps, thorn scrub and empty glare, should sprawl heedlessly across as many miles as it needed. Then let the veld resume once more, in every direction – pale, flat, untilled, ragged, silent.

For two or three years we moved from house to house, until we arrived at the veranda-encircled dwelling which remained in

71

the family's possession for the next forty years. To me – just days after we had arrived in Kimberley – it was if I had lived in the town for ever. Of what had preceded our arrival I had only a few fragmentary memories, each isolated from the others, curtained around by darkness. Now everything suddenly revealed itself to be connected with everything else. Places were connected spatially; events temporally; people in terms of what they did and whether or not they were members of the family. These were the roads that took me to town and brought me back from it; this event happened before or after that one; Dora cooked for us, Sannie polished the floors, David worked in the garden. My mother and father went in their car to work every day.

And so forth. In fact, the society in which we had found ourselves was quite as fissured as any to be found in Lithuania, and (for the blacks) almost as comprehensively ruled by administrative fiat. Thirty years before our arrival in Kimberley the Anglo-Boer War had been fought to decide which of the country's two white groups should be masters of the subcontinent. The town itself was hardly more than sixty years old when we moved there. The mixture of peoples around us – English-speaking and Afrikaans-speaking whites, Cape Coloureds, blacks of different tribal origins, Indians, Chinese and a variety of other, still smaller groups – had come into existence as the result of a 'rush' to the diamond fields, which had not only long since petered out but had been replaced by a steady loss of numbers. As if in defiance of the normal laws of physics, the city appeared to be made up of many mutually exclusive zones, defined by colour, origin and language, which did not merely overlap with one another but filled the same spaces simultaneously. Any step you made in any direction passed through them all; and yet left you exactly where you had been before.

None of this, however, prevented me from regarding the Kimberley of my childhood as a place of unshakeable antiquity, or its social arrangements as fixed more or less permanently in the forms they had assumed. There was no questioning that the dominant group in the city then, politically and culturally (and hence morally too), was the British. Whether colonial or 'home'-born, they ran the show; the latter among them especially. Somehow for *them* to have migrated to South Africa, however humble their circumstances might now be, was perceived by them (and others) almost as an act of *noblesse oblige*; for my parents to have done so, however, marked them down for ever as 'foreigners'.

This is not an autobiography. Of the many threads that run through my earliest years, I intend to follow only one: that of the connection I had, or did not have, to the distant part of the world my parents had come from.

No sooner do I pull at that particular thread, however, than much of my childhood seems to snag tightly around it. The years are drawn into a knot that was impossible for me to undo then and is difficult enough for me to loosen even now. Whenever I thought about the unimaginable regions where my dead grandfather lay, the emotions I chiefly felt were fear, bewilderment and something resembling pity. Disbelief too: at finding myself linked so closely to a world so strange to me which had yet produced the parents I knew, loved, admired, depended on – and whom I wished I could change from what they were.

It was because they had come from Lithuania and Latvia, respectively, and because of the religion and way of life that had dominated their parents' lives there, that our family was 'different', marked out, exposed to the special hostility or curiosity of many of the people around us. The Yiddish language, which my parents often used in speaking to one another, though to us they spoke only English, was another aspect of our differentness. So was the fact that their English did not sound like that spoken by the parents of other boys at school.

So were the prayers muttered or chanted at the synagogue which my father intermittently demanded we should attend; so were the afternoon lessons in Hebrew which he more persistently urged us to go to.

And for what? Out of respect for a commanding, interested, *choosing* God I did not believe in and (looking back) seem never to have believed in, even momentarily? For a history I had not volunteered to be a part of? (As if any of us volunteer for the parents we have and the circumstances in which we are born to them.) Out of loyalty to habits established in an 'old country' I thought of not only as remote, but backward, poverty-stricken, prison-like? From my parents I knew it to be a place where the Jews did not attend schools that 'everyone' attended (bar the blacks of course), as I did; where they did not speak the language spoken by 'everyone' (who mattered), as I did; where they were not permitted to become doctors or lawyers or scientists, as I could, if I wished; where nobody had the vote, nobody went to the movies, nobody had a telephone; where nobody played rugby, cricket or tennis. Above all, perhaps, it was a country where English – the language of the dominant group, the mark of our status as British subjects (in those late-imperial days) and our passport to a sophisticated, worldwide culture – was not spoken.

Obviously I did not explicitly think of the English language in these terms. But I knew well enough how important it was, not least because I was surrounded by so many people who did not have it. However much I may have taken Kimberley for granted, and relished the freedom of its open spaces (in those days the unfenced veld began not fifty yards from our front garden), I acquired at an early age a sense that the town we lived in was a shabby, bypassed place even within South Africa, let alone in its relation to the larger world. I soon learned to hanker after other countries and continents, even other centuries: those I read about in books and comics, or saw versions of in the local cinemas, or heard about on the radio. But it was in English, always, that my hankerings were schooled, and in English that their eventual or possible satisfaction was intimated to me.

For Lithuania I never hankered. If anything, it was like a wound within me. So far from being a country to which my childhood longings and ambitions could attach themselves, it was the place my mother had escaped from: nothing else; nothing more. The same applied to Latvia, my father's country of origin, which he had left many years before her departure from Europe. I can remember the shock I felt, at about the age of seven, two or three years before the outbreak of the Second World War, when I learned that my father's much older and wealthier brother had gone 'home' with his family for a brief visit there – i.e. on a *holiday.* It seemed to me uncanny that he should have done so: as if, say, a meteorite should suddenly start up from the spot on earth on which it had fallen and make its way back to the moon or Mars or somewhere even further afield.

The peasants, woods and snows my parents sometimes spoke of may have sounded exotic; but they made no appeal to me. Their exoticism was indistinguishable from too many of its dire accompaniments: pogroms when Jews were attacked; *yeshivas* where they studied nothing but the Talmud and swayed for ever over dusty Bibles and prayer books; *shtetls* where they huddled together for comfort in the midst of a great darkness. Stark hunger, through much of my father's childhood, had been another accompaniment too. That my mother's father should actually have chosen to remain in those bleak territories, though he had been given the opportunity to move to the United States – a country where they made movies, where they made Buicks, where they built skyscrapers and spoke English – struck me, when I heard about it, as bizarre and incomprehensible; even mad. Or if that was too strong, then revelatory of the unfathom-able strangeness of the place he had lived in, the people he had shared it with, and his own stern nature.

To put it bluntly: like most Jews of my generation I believed that our parents and grandparents had come from Nowhere. They might occasionally refer to *der heim* in affectionately sentimental terms; they might even try to remind us that Vilnius had been so great a centre of Jewish learning it had gone by the name of the 'Jerusalem of the north'. Yet none of them wanted to go back there. So we knew we were right to think of it as we did. In migrating from Lithuania to South Africa they had moved from Nowhere to Somewhere.

It never occurred to us that in certain respects the opposite may have been true: that they had actually exchanged Some-where for Nowhere. (I know many people who find it impossible to believe still.) We could not imagine that Jewish Vilnius and Kaunas – I specifically exclude here, as I must, the riches of their then-predominant Polish and Russian cultures – might have been centres of a high civilization, compared with anything the immigrants would find in Johannesburg and Cape Town. Let alone in comparison with what awaited them in the tiny, lost-in-space *dorps* in the backveld, where so many of them first made their homes.

Perhaps I would have felt differently if I had grown up in a city like Johannesburg, in which Jews made up a substantial part of the city's white population. But I grew up where I did: in a town with a small Jewish population (about 120 families, at most, none of them related to us). Moreover, this was at a time when Jews everywhere were being subjected to a worldwide, systematic campaign of vilification, originating in Nazi Germany and unprecedented in scale and degree of malevolence. Its effects were manifest in Kimberley too – at school, in the streets, in the newspapers. Every anti-Semitic jeer or threat I encountered was like a burn on my consciousness, for which no remedy or redress could be found, since it had nothing to do with what I actually did and everything to do with what I undeniably was. Still, when I look back on that period, when one of the world's great powers was tirelessly devoting the resources of its propaganda machine (itself a brand-new invention) to the spreading of crazy lies about the Jews, I am now faintly surprised at how peacefully we lived, at how much respect was shown to my father in the town, at how many of my closest friends were gentiles.

So I am not interested in telling a hard-luck story here. Rather, the point I want to make reaches as deeply as anything can into my relations with my parents, my grandparents in Johannesburg and my solitary grandfather left behind in Lithuania. It is this. Everything I have so far said describes my childhood feelings about Lithuania *before* the outbreak of the Second World War; or at any rate before we knew the full extent of what was being done to the Jews of Europe during the war. Even in those pre-war days – I will not call them innocent – Lithuania had essentially been for me a country to abjure. In so far as it was inhabited by gentiles, it was an arena of deprivation and threat. In so far as it was inhabited by Jews, it belonged to what the Russian Jewish poet Osip Mandelstam called 'the Talmudic wilds' – a region darker in my imagination than anything I was likely to see around me in the sandy, suburban Africa I knew best.

In *The Noise of Time*, the memoir of his assimilated, middle-class childhood in St Petersburg from which I have just quoted, Mandelstam also described the Jewish Latvia of his parents as 'not a motherland, not a house, not a hearth, but precisely a chaos, the unknown womb world whence I had issued, which I feared, about which I made vague conjectures and fled'.

When I read those words for the first time they evoked in me a feeling stronger than recognition. It was as if this man, about whose work and life I had previously known nothing, was uncannily articulating some of my own earliest and least expressible memories.

During my childhood we used to go up to Johannesburg about twice a year. We generally lodged in private hotels or boarding houses in the suburb of Hillbrow, where my grandmother shared a flat with her unmarried daughters. That part of the city has since fallen on bad times; its streets are now given over to prostitution, crime, drugs, street children, beggars, muggers, strip joints, tattoo parlours, porn shops (pawnshops too) and gutted, squatted or vandalized apartment blocks. It was quite different then: a casual mixture of low, iron-roofed cottages, modestly aspiring blocks of flats (eight or ten storeys high) and a few streets of down-at-heel but entirely respectable shops and cafés. In those days every tenant, shopkeeper or homeowner was white, aside from some Indians and Chinese; the only blacks to be seen were in domestic or commercial employment in the district. To the north, each astride its own ridge, were the wealthy suburbs of Houghton and Parktown; to the south, no more than a mile away, was the skyline of the city's central business district, where many lofty buildings were topped by red, white, blue and green neon signs that did amazing things – poured drinks from bottles, sent stick men dancing from left to right and back again, wiped themselves out in elaborate ways and reappeared the moment the task was done. Behind them, shaped like whales or ocean liners, but looking much older than the city itself and bigger by far than any of its buildings, were the white and yellow dumps from the gold mines.

To me, coming from drought-stricken, backward Kimberley, it was all amazing. Such a multiplicity of streets and shops! Such green trees along the pavements! Such steep hills and valleys everywhere! So many traffic lights to control the ever-arriving cars! So many tall buildings, each with its oiled, humming lift making a different noise and smelling a little differently from the last or next! The certainty that I would never again see most of the faces that passed! It was especially thrilling to stand in the early evenings on the balcony of my grandmother's flat (first in a block called Belmont Court; later in one by the name of Rockridge Heights) and look at the unexpected angles and patterns made by the streets below, and the busy foreshortened passers-by who did not know that they were being watched, while the noise of the city rose in a hiss and murmur to the sky. Intermittently all of it would crystallize into a single event, a gathered-together image and sound: a man shouting on a street corner, the crack and flash of fierce blue electricity from a turning tram in Kotze Street, a car lurching and squealing as it braked.

Then I would go indoors, into the lit-up space in which my young aunts and old grandmother had made their home. A different kind of glamour awaited me there. To be living in a flat, so high above the ground and identical to those above it and below it, seemed in itself magical and metropolitan to me. So did the youth of my aunts Zippy and Reevee, and of Sadie too, who was by then already married but lived nearby and was a frequent visitor. (Doomed Rae, with her unstable, poetry-loving husband who was to kill himself a few years later, and the unsuspected heart condition that was to carry her off not long afterwards, should have belonged to this group, but was always an outsider to it.) They were all slim, talkative, smartly dressed; they spoke in an English that had no trace of their

Lithuanian origin; they smoked cigarettes; they wore elaborate make-up and smelled of perfume as well as cigarette smoke; they greeted one another and their visiting nephews and niece from Kimberley with loud cries of 'Darling!'; they worked in offices in the centre of town and remained there all day; in the evenings they went out on their mysterious, grown-up engagements. In manner and appearance they were quite unlike my plump, reserved, bespectacled mother; yet they were 'hers', and therefore the allurements and mysteries of their early womanhood were 'mine' too.

And yet not mine. From an early age I was uneasily aware that my mother, who was the oldest of the children, behaved in a deferential, even subservient, manner to all her brothers and sisters. She agreed with everything they said; she could not bear to hear a word of criticism uttered against them; even our childish attempts at imitating their voices and mannerisms were suppressed with an uncharacteristic severity. To this day it remains a mystery to me why her attachment to them should have been so self-abasing, especially as I never felt that they reciprocated her devotion with anything like the fervour she showed towards them. For this reason, among others, I am convinced that had her father lived nothing would have persuaded her to leave her family behind in Lithuania. She was incapable of it. Even Kimberley, 300 miles away, was further from them than she could really bear to be.

In the middle of all this was my grandmother Menuchah, relict of the late Rabbi Heshel Melamed of Varniai. She looked so old when I first became aware of her that I had no sense of her becoming older still as the years passed. She was old, she always had been old, she always would be, and that was that. Now I wonder at my own impercipience, at my inability to register how much she must have changed while I was growing up. The grandmother who lived in a flat in Hillbrow, Johannesburg, with her two youngest daughters, could not have been the same person I saw for the last time in a Jewish old-age home in a different suburb of the city: that is now plain to me. But try as I might I cannot *see* the difference in my memories of her; only the different circumstances in which she was placed.

More than just her age and her piety, however, set her apart from the daughters with whom she lived. They were voluble; she was quiet. They were demonstrative; she always kept her emotions under restraint. In dress and manner they made the most of themselves; she invariably wore a widow's subfusc. She was pious and observant; they were the reverse (though respectful of her rules within the flat). One would never have known that they had ever lived in distant Lithuania; there was something in her proud, dry, self-deprecatory air that suggested she was living there still.

Yet no matter how bowed her shoulders became, and how subdued she had schooled her gestures and expressions to be, she always kept her head bravely tilted upwards and her small face fully exposed to the world. After her death – like most grandchildren, I suspect – I wished that I had spoken more to her when I had had the chance to do so, and had made more of an effort to get her to speak to me. However, the difference in age between us was not all that kept us apart; language was a greater barrier still. She was an assiduous reader of newspapers and listener to news broadcasts; but she was embarrassed by the deficiencies of her spoken English. For similar but inverse reasons she found it humiliating to speak to us in Yiddish, knowing that some or much of what she said might be passing us by. I would see the discomfort and sadness of it on her features, especially when she felt impelled to turn to one of her children to translate her remarks to us. (Unnecessarily, sometimes.) Our ignorance of many aspects of Jewish law was also a source of despondency and vexation to her. She was aware, of course, that her own children never went to *shul* and were 'observant' only when they were in her presence. But at least they knew what it was that they had turned their backs on. But us? Her grandchildren? We were too ignorant even to know the nature of our loss.

She could hardly have guessed that, on our side, we felt there to be something intimidating about her *frumkeit*, her strict adherence to the observances of her religion. Frail and out of date she might have been, yet her piety was a constant reminder to us that she had a will of her own: that she was a devoted keeper of the flame; a zealous executor, in a country he never wanted her to live in, of her dead husband's wishes.

After the last of her daughters had married, the flat in Rockridge Heights was given up and Menuchah moved to a rented room in a house belonging to a woman who was not much younger than herself and as scrupulously orthodox. Unlike Menuchah, however, her landlady was fortunate enough to have in tow a diminished, docile, bearded husband. I do not know whether my grandmother ever ate with this couple or confined herself to what she could cook on the little electric hotplate in a corner of her room. In another corner, prominently displayed in its wooden sarcophagus, like a memorial of domesticities abandoned but not forgotten, was the hand-driven Singer sewing machine she had once busily plied. She had her own bathroom and a window that overlooked the back yard and the servants' quarters.

She was still occupying that room when I came to live in Johannesburg as a university student. During my first year I boarded in a house just a few blocks from her; even then I seldom went to see her unless my mother was in town or some other member of the family took me there. I have distinct memories of three of the visits I made to her in that room. The first arose by accident. We met in the street on a Saturday morning, when she and her landlady were walking back from the nearest *shul*. Both were wearing black dresses; on my grandmother's head was a little straw hat with a veil, also black, like a boater in mourning; they moved along the pavement in a manner that was cautious yet dignified, even procession-like. (For 'security reasons' it would probably be unthinkable in today's Johannesburg for two such well-dressed, handbag-carrying old ladies to walk on their own down any suburban street, at any time.) Clearly I had *not* been to *shul*, and the landlady could not restrain herself from saying so. Menuchah touched her on the arm lightly and briefly, as a way of telling her to leave me alone. I walked back with them to the house; during the minutes I spent subsequently in her room she showed me, perhaps by way of a follow-up to the little three-way exchange that had just taken place, Heshel Melamed's *machzor* (prayer book). Holding the thick, square, leather-bound book he had handled daily, looking at its pages crowded with a heavy black Hebrew print I could read but of which I could understand relatively little, I felt with equal acuteness both the absence and the presence of the dead man. Dust-tainted rays of sunlight fell into the back yard. I asked her what he had been like. 'A good man,' she replied. 'A very learned man.'

She spoke sincerely; yet her answer succeeded in stifling rather than satisfying my curiosity. Perhaps it was intended to do that. She stretched out a hand complicated by veins, knots of bone and a single gold ring to take the prayer book from me. This was just a year or two after the end of the Second World War. Much detailed information about Nazi crimes in Europe had still to emerge, but their nature and extent had been written about, spoken of and displayed on cinema screens all over the world. I knew that she had recently had precise news of the extent of her own losses in Lithuania. She never uttered a word to me about them. She never would.

I will have more to say of them later.

*

84

Around that time, before the State of Israel had come into existence, various armed Jewish underground organizations were waging a fierce struggle against the British colonial administration which then ruled Palestine. I had long known that she was as strongly anti-Zionist as her husband had been, and therefore did not expect her to have any sympathy with the Jewish gunmen or their objectives. What I did not expect, however, when I visited her in that room on another occasion, was the passionate defence of British institutions and the English language into which she – in her broken English – launched herself. What had provoked her to speak in this way I cannot now remember. During her lifetime, she told me, it was in countries where English was spoken, in countries that had got their systems of government and law from Britain, that Jews had been allowed to live in peace. *Only* in such places had mass anti-Semitic political movements never appeared. Go to the United States, go to Britain, to Canada, to Australia – the same thing applied. Was that an accident? Of course not. It was because of the laws, the books, the parliaments, the constitutions, that went with the language. And here were these crazy people in Palestine killing Englishmen. No good would come of it.

Finally, on a later visit to that room I had the shock of finding her son Michael sitting in it. It came as a shock to me because he had been banished from her presence after his marriage to an Afrikaner by the name of Joey (Johanna). His marrying 'out' had so upset her that we had been told never to mention his name in her presence. Ditto Joey's, of course. And double or quadruple ditto the names of the two sons whom Joey had produced for him. Of their very existence she was supposed to be completely ignorant.

Yet there he was, the banished, apostate son, the former *yeshiva* runaway, a scapegrace still, sitting on a low chair not three feet from her, his hands on his thighs and his elbows cocked outwards, as they always were, talking as vehemently as he always did and interrupting himself even more frequently than usual with his bark-like laugh. Listening to him, I soon realized that this rapprochement with his mother, however it may have come about, still did not permit him to mention Joey or his sons to her.

Subsequently I used to see him quite often in her company; but the existence of his family remained taboo for her until her death. I remember one excruciating occasion when a misunderstanding brought her to Leib's flat when Michael's sons also happened to be there. On some pretext or other, which she knew to be a pretext, she was kept waiting in the car while the two crop-headed, naked-eared boys were rushed out of the back entrance to the little apartment block. When this had been done and a determinedly inconscient Menuchah was safely indoors, the youngsters returned, pitifully enough, to peer through the outside window at the grandmother they had never seen before and who supposedly did not know that they existed. Their eyes and the top of their small blond heads appeared and disappeared at a windowsill a few yards from her; but she remained invincibly ignorant of their presence.

Decades later my aunt Zippy said to me fiercely, not about that particular incident but about the entire conspiracy of silence regarding these two grandchildren, 'It was all so stupid! We should never have tolerated all that nonsense from her!'

But they did.

Menuchah lost her rented room when her landlady's husband died and the house was sold. She then moved to a Jewish old-age home in Norwood: an institution erected not long before and intended chiefly for elderly refugees from Germany. It was complete with lawns, verandas, lifts, activity rooms, a lecture hall, special bathrooms and lavatories for the infirm, notice-boards, meetings and many kindly-looking African nurses and cleaners. Her son Leib had had to use his influence as an officer of the South African Jewish Board of Deputies to get her into it, such was the demand for places there; and her daughters and sons-in-law dipped deeply into their pockets to cover the costs.

She never liked the place. It was not a home; not even a shadow of a home, like the one she had just given up. The people around her were German Jews ('*yekkes*'), not Litvaks like herself. She said there was no one to talk to, though the few times I visited her I thought the other inmates appeared to treat her respectfully enough. Also, the religious ethos of the place, so far as it had one, was insufficiently strict for her; she suspected it of being infected by the 'reform' practices characteristic of German Jewry. But there she had to remain, in a room of her own, with her bits and pieces around her and a window overlooking a *donga*, along which straggled small acacias and gum trees. I saw her there for the last time one autumn afternoon. By then I had graduated, spent almost two years in Israel and Europe, and come back to work as a journalist in Johannesburg. She described the whole place to me (in English) as 'a dressed-up waiting room' – a vivid, sardonic phrase which left me feeling that she had made up her mind to face what was coming in undaunted fashion.

Not long afterwards I returned to England, which then became my permanent home. What happened to Menuchah subsequently I heard about from my mother. The very last period of her life was not resigned, not comforted by the faith she had clung to with such tenacity. On the contrary. As she became weaker, she became increasingly filled with a fear of dying, of death, of being punished in that afterlife which my mother was doubtful that Heshel Melamed, her rabbinical father, had ever fully believed in. I do not know the exact form her fears took; or whether the obsessional anxieties she had developed were connected in any way with her life as a married woman, or with her children's multiple lapses of faith, or with the fate that had befallen her brother and sisters and their children who had remained in Kelme, Lithuania. Perhaps, ironically enough, she blamed herself for not having made sufficient effort to bring them out to South Africa when there had been time to do so.

All that is just guesswork on my part. What I do know is that there is something peculiarly hateful in the thought of a person who was so little given to emotional display, and who had suffered so many losses, early and late, being reduced to such a condition at the end of her life. Eventually her depression and terror became so extreme that she was taken out of the home and handed over to a psychiatric hospital where – and I find this hard to credit, though I know my mother would never have invented such a tale – she was given electroconvulsive 'therapy'.

How her children could have permitted this to be done to so frail a creature, at so advanced an age, I cannot imagine. Or rather I can – just. They were all inclined to an excessive credulity before the wonderful powers of modern medicine.

Then she died, Heshel Melamed's second wife, mother of his nine children. Eight of those children, several of whom were then in a pretty woebegone condition themselves, for a variety of reasons, were left to mourn her going. And doubtless also to feel some relief that the mental sufferings she had been going through were at last over.

[9]

I have written of South Africa as a haven of safety and a land of opportunity for the Jews who had come to live there. So it was: within limits. Politically speaking the country I grew up in was a strange hybrid. For the whites it had every appearance of being a genuine British-style democracy, complete with the king of England as its monarch, 'universal' suffrage, several competing political parties, an independent judiciary, a press expressing a wide range of opinions, autonomous religious bodies and independent professional and voluntary organizations of all kinds. These freedoms and privileges were not available to the blacks, however. Even in those days, long before the introduction of apartheid by the Afrikaner Nationalists, they were governed by an oppressive administrative apparatus which tried to keep under control almost every aspect of their lives – where they could work, where they could own property, what jobs they could do, the kind of education they were entitled to receive, their right to join political parties and trade unions.

Few South African whites found it morally objectionable that two or three million of them should hold in subjection four or five times that number of blacks. Far from it. Especially as the course of South African history had ensured that every group in the country felt entitled to regard itself as threatened by all the others, separately or jointly. This applied quite as much to the top dogs then (the British) as it did to those at the bottom of the heap (the blacks). Most of the Afrikaners (descendants of the Boers, and the majority group among the whites) saw themselves as having been cruelly dispossessed of their land and self-respect by the British. The fact that over the previous three centuries they had themselves dispossessed and subjugated a variety of competing black tribes merely made them fear and despise the latter even more intensely than they might otherwise have done.

As for the Jews, their prominence in the development of the diamond and gold fields had done nothing to make them popular among either Britons or Boers. The Afrikaner Nationalist Party, which was much the strongest movement among the latter, became deeply influenced by Nazi propaganda and ideology during the 1930s, and strongly opposed South Africa's entering the Second World War on the side of the Allies. Most of its members rejoiced in every German success on the western and eastern fronts between 1939 and 1941. They also made no secret of their intention to do their worst by the Jews, once the triumph of Hitler's Reich had finally come about.

I was a child when the war began and an adolescent when it ended, but none of this was hidden from me. Of course nobody knew then what 'the worst' could mean in this context: not even, I am sure, most of the people who looked forward to a German victory. The Jews feared that were a Nationalist administration to come into office in the wake of an Allied surrender, it would behave as the Nazis had done in Germany before the war. They foresaw officially sponsored pogroms, expropriations of Jewish property, expulsions of Jews from jobs and schools, even perhaps the expulsion of the entire community from the country itself. I can remember listening to a conversation between my father and his brother-in-law, my uncle Leib, during one of our family visits to Johannesburg, which must have taken place at about the time of the fall of France in 1940. Leib was distraught, convinced that all was lost, even in tears at one stage; my father, on the other hand, took on the role of the strong man, the propper-up of morale, the one who was convinced that 'a mad dog' like Hitler would be bound to bring about his own destruction sooner or later.

Yet I can also remember him reading to my mother, with a shaking voice, a report from one of the South African Jewish newspapers about the mass killings of Jews just behind the German lines on the eastern front. This, I now realize, must have been more than two years after that conversation with Leib, as it was not until late in 1942 that reliable accounts of what was being done to the Jews in eastern Europe began to be published in the general press. In fact those accounts lagged far behind the events they attempted to describe. The extermination of the overwhelming majority of Lithuanian and Latvian Jews was already 'history' by then; it had been completed a full twelve months before the first, attenuated accounts of the events were made public. The seemingly unreal or quasi-fictional quality of the reports which appeared in piecemeal fashion over the following years did nothing to diminish their horror. On the contrary, it was a part of their horror, and has remained so ever since. To this day we find ourselves in the impossible position of being unable to accept imaginatively, let alone understand, something which we know as certainly as we know our own names and addresses to have taken place. What is more, this was true even *for them*: by which I mean that there is ample evidence of the extent to which the Nazis were helped in the execution of their crimes by the victims' stark inability to believe – until it was too late – that these people literally intended to kill every single one of them.

But they did. They would have killed us all in South Africa too, if they could have reached us.

When the Afrikaner Nationalists finally came to power in

1948, three years after the end of the war, they attempted to turn the 'traditional', haphazard forms of white domination and social segregation which had long been practised in South Africa into a doctrine: universal, systematic, elaborated, fiercely enforced, oriented towards a future which would find room for nothing but itself – for ever. That Hitlerian ideas of racial purity and superiority lay not far behind much of their legislation was apparent. But by then a programmatic anti-Semitism had lost its éclat even for them.

I cannot remember the exact stages through which I learned the truth – or as much of it as I could or wished to assimilate – about what had happened to the Jews in occupied Europe. No doubt it came to me by way of the usual mixture of cinema newsreels, newspaper reports, accounts of the Nuremberg trials of the Nazi leaders and so forth. What I do know is that by the time the war had ended, or soon afterwards, it had become impossible for me to think of the world my parents had lived in, the world my grandfather had chosen to live in, as anything but a locus of terror, a hole in space and time from which no hope, light or reason could ever emerge.

Nor could any redeeming, comprehending or re-creative impulse penetrate that region from the outside. Not only the present and future of Jewish life had been annihilated there, but also its entire past. It was to *this*, we now knew, that more than seven centuries of east European Jewish life had been secretly moving: this was the climax of its history, its target or *telos*; this was how it had always been doomed to end. Or so it seemed. How pale and beside the point it now was to think of the region, as I had previously done, in terms of mere backwardness and deprivation, religious obscurantism and random persecution. All these, which I had been so conscious of during my childhood, had become as nothing. Only a consciousness of the catastrophe remained: an event it was impossible to think about, or around, or through, or (so to speak) behind.

It was not until the war was over that my grandmother Menuchah learned exactly when, where and how her brother, her two sisters and their families in the town of Kelme had been murdered, along with everyone else she had left behind – the playmates of her childhood, the companions of her youth, the friends of her adulthood. It seems amazing to me now that neither my older brothers nor I have any recollection of her ever referring to the fate of her family: not during the war, when she must have lived in a daily turmoil of ignorance about what was happening to them; not afterwards, when ignorance had been replaced by a merciless certainty. I suspect that even to say the names of the victims to us, who had never known them, to whom they would never *be* anything but names, was more than she could bear. Nor were we told that for some years afterwards she kept alive a hopeless hope that her sister Merre's children – 'the boys', as they were called by my aunts – might somehow have escaped. Naturally her children were much more aware than we were of the griefs which she suffered during the war and after it; but long after their mother's death they too remained remarkably silent on the subject. In fact they barely referred to it any more than their mother had done. It was locked away.

So, in effect, was Lithuania: the country they had been born in and had been fortunate enough to leave. It too was locked away from outside scrutiny; it was sealed off from the world almost as tightly as it had been during the war. Once the Germans had left, taking with them many of their local henchmen, who now passed themselves off as pitiful refugees, victims of Nazism, worthy applicants for admission to the United States, Australia or Great Britain, the Communists moved in.

Another pit. Another falling out of reach. Entire peoples put once again into the hands of grubby functionaries whose years of active service as mass murderers for Stalin might have been drawing to an end, but whose power continued to be limited only by the power of the yet grubbier functionaries placed above them. Servants of the regime, they remained the masters still: party members; secret policemen; labour-camp kings; movers-about of papers and populations, governors of a realm where the individual had no recourse against state and party – not at work, not in the law courts, not even with his family or among his friends, who could themselves be party functionaries without anyone else knowing it.

And this stifled, ramshackle, half-lit realm of lies and unfreedom, to which entry was forbidden, from which escape was forbidden, managing to sustain itself and to threaten others for decade after decade. Leaving me, like most of the people I knew, convinced that it would still be there, more or less unaltered, long after my own life had ended.

In spite of which I discovered in myself, as the years passed, a growing desire to visit my mother's country of birth. It became stronger still after her death in Kimberley. I had not felt it as a child, but I was a child no longer. In any case its pressure was stronger than that of mere wish or curiosity. It felt like an obligation, even a compulsion.

I made my first attempts to get to Lithuania when it was still a province or colony – a 'federated state', officially – of the Soviet Union. For reasons known only to themselves, the Soviet authorities had declared the whole of Lithuania to be a 'military area', along with Latvia and Estonia. They were closed to visitors from the West. Only especially privileged diplomats or businessmen were permitted to enter them. This policy remained in force for thirty years or longer. In the declining years of the Communist regime, however, brief guided tours of the region began to be offered to foreign visitors. If they bought a package which included Leningrad, for instance, they were permitted to spend a night in each of the Baltic's three capital cities, Riga, Tallinn and Vilnius.

This concession encouraged me to apply for something more ambitious. (By then I had been living in London for many years.) My aim was to be allowed to spend several days in Lithuania and to travel to the places which most interested me, my grandfather's Varniai and my great-grandfather's Kelme especially. People I consulted who were experienced in dealing with the ways of the Soviet authorities advised me to broach the project through the Soviet Writers' Union; or, failing that, the Lithuanian Writers' Union. The approaches I made along these lines produced only delays and double talk. After much badgering, each of the unions referred me to the other – twice over. Then both took shelter behind the cultural attaché of the Soviet embassy in London, who responded to my letters and phone calls by blandly referring me back to where I had already been. Eventually I simply gave up the plan, as they no doubt intended me to.

When the revolution in eastern Europe took place in the late 1980s, I found myself set free, like any other Westerner, to go to Lithuania whenever I wished. By that time, however, I had also been set free (in a different sense) by the parallel revolution in South Africa to take up another self-imposed, long-deferred obligation I had been waiting to discharge. I wanted to travel along, and to write about, a corridor once known as the 'missionary road' which ran for much of its length along the eastern edge of the Kalahari Desert. During the late-imperial 'Scramble for Africa' this route was thought to be of crucial strategic importance by all the parties struggling to control the interior of the continent – British, Boers, Tswana, Ndebele, Germans, Portuguese. Subsequently it had dropped completely out of everyone's awareness.

My home town, Kimberley, had been the anchor and jumping-off place for the missionary road; yet I had seen virtually nothing of the territories it passed through. The sense of a huge, barely inhabited region so close to where I lived, and yet so dreamlike in its remoteness, had always been lodged in my childhood consciousness. There were spaces up there (and in me) that I had long wanted to fill. Now that the blight of apartheid had been lifted from both South Africa and the countries around it, it was possible for me to take up the project at last.

Only after my travels along the missionary road had been done, and I had written my book about it (*The Electronic Elephant*), could I think again of visiting Lithuania. Like the deserts to the north of Kimberley, it too had always been a part of my consciousness.

A different part. A darker and more sinister *terra incognita*. One that was lightless, unmoving, at the centre of everything else. Around it there revolved, sometimes more obtrusively, sometimes less so, thoughts which were not-thoughts, feelings which were not-feelings, understandings which were not and never will be understandings.

At the very least I wanted to establish the physical reality of the country. That was my first wish, my prime intention, once I began to take seriously the prospect of going there. From infancy onwards the five melodious syllables of its name, Lith-u-a-ni-a, rising towards their long, central 'a' and then falling away from it, and always accompanied by harsh, brief discords like Vorna, Kelm and Trishick, had made a strange music in my ears. Approaching the other end of my life, I wanted to transform those sounds into things at once more substantial and more banal: streets, buildings, countryside, people, trees, farms, railway sidings. What did they look like? What would it feel like to be there? How much of it would I recognize? These were the dauntingly simple-minded questions about my mother's 'homeland' I wanted to have answered.

Now that I have been there, I understand better than before the peculiar force those questions had for me. I felt as I did because I could not imagine there would be anything but the physical aspect of the country for me to encounter. What else could there be? People? The people I was connected with – and the people *they* had been connected with – had all been killed. (Not a single member of my mother's family who was alive in Lithuania at the time of the German invasion, and whose name was known to those living in South Africa, survived. Not an uncle, an aunt, a cousin, a second cousin. And had I belonged to a wholly different family, which had also had kinsmen left behind, I would almost certainly have had to write exactly the same words about them.) Institutions? They had all been destroyed. Buildings? They had all been burned down. Or they were now in the hands of strangers who would steadfastly know nothing about the previous owners.

The poet Edward Thomas, writing shortly before his death in the trenches of the First World War, had told me what kind of lesson the place might offer:

> I learned how the wind would sound
> After these things should be.

Lithuania's tourist trade, I discovered while I was there, seemed to consist chiefly of tiny handfuls of Jews (of the three groups I met, two were from South Africa) wandering around in search of what they called their 'roots'. I understood this search, even felt myself to be taking part in it, and yet understood it not at all. What 'roots'? Regardless of the centuries that had passed since the arrival of their forebears in Lithuania, the Jews had never felt themselves to be truly rooted in it. Everything that was their own – their holy texts, prayers, rituals, languages, folk memories, foods, festivals and calendar, not to speak of an ever-present sense of their own vulnerability – had constantly reminded them that their roots were elsewhere: in a land from which the God of Israel had banished them and to which he would bring them back at the end of history. It was that sense of suspension and expectation which, precisely and paradoxically, had been their true abode: the timeless space, the spaceless time, which my grandfather had wanted to preserve in its purity until divine intervention replaced it with something better.

Unlike Heshel Melamed, tens of thousands of others had allowed themselves to be driven by necessity or lured by opportunities elsewhere to leave Lithuania. No subsequent act of will or impulse of sentiment on the part of their children, grandchildren, great-grandchildren could undo the changes produced in them by that 'primal' act of emigration to the United States, Britain, Israel, the Argentine, South Africa. Even in the best of circumstances no one could ever climb back up that ladder again.

But these were now and henceforth always would be the worst of circumstances. The country which the emigrants had left behind was no longer just a geographical and political entity. It had become instead one of the names – one of the hundreds, even thousands of names – given to an unparalleled catastrophe.

Is is possible to have 'roots' in such an abyss? I think not.

My father's Latvia had never roused the same curiosity in me as had my mother's Lithuania. It had always been her country, her *shtetl*, that I wanted to visit. In large part, I know, this was because of the phantasmal relationship I had had with my missing grandfather, Heshel Melamed. It was his *absence* that for so long had made him an unsettling and magnetic 'presence' for me; just as the knowledge that he would have kept my mother in deadly Lithuania, for religion's sake, had filled me with the kind of disbelief and bewilderment of which I have spoken earlier. Of him alone among my four grandparents could I have said that he had helped to bring me into existence and also done his utmost to prevent my coming into existence.

Therefore I wanted to visit him. He was the one I had to go looking for.

I must speak carefully here, though. When I set out for Lithuania I had no hope – not even of the most fanciful kind – of meeting anyone who remembered him or would know anything about him; or of stumbling on a set of documents which would clear up puzzling aspects of his life and character. (Those three names of his, for example, or his two marriages.) Nor did I expect to come on any physical marker or reminder of him. How could even the frailest hopes of this kind be nourished so long after his death, and in a region where so many memories, an entire nation of memories, had been effaced?

So things turned out, in effect. In going to Lithuania I did succeed in transforming familiar words and place-names into visible, palpable, even smellable facts. But everything about Heshel Melamed as an individual that had been hidden from me before I went there remains hidden still, and always will do so. His secrets are enclosed in time past like the pattern inside an uncut agate stone: not just beyond amendment or erasure, but unknowable too.

So this is not a story in which a series of riddles is proposed in order to have them resolved in the last chapter, as in a detective novel. Nor is it one of a mystical reunion beyond the grave. On the other hand, I did learn something about my grandfather I had not expected beforehand; it had not even occurred to me that it might be possible to do so. Looking about me in Lithuania, searching for him in the midst of a devastating absence and emptiness, I was surprised to find myself grasping for the first time the full reality *to itself* of the obliterated community he had belonged to. Seeing him in the context of his vanished people, of the nation that now is not, I began to understand for the first time how it could once have seemed to him sufficient; as much as he needed; as much as a man like himself could expect to find on God's unredeemed earth.

There was also one specific, family obligation I undertook in going to Lithuania. To explain it I must return to my uncle Leib, who has been glimpsed here at various stages in his career: as reluctant *yeshiva bocher* in Lithuania, as Hebrew teacher in his earliest days in Johannesburg and as an old, ill man living with his daughter and son-in-law in Warwickshire, England.

Some time before he reached that last stage, I happened to be the only member of the family available when he suffered a severe mental collapse. He was then living alone. At one point in the wretchedly protracted drama which followed – with its manias, prostrations, self-injuries, hospitalizations, break-outs, overdoses, 'sectioning' and much else besides – I was obliged to clear his things from the rented room he had been living in. He was present as I went about the task, but was incapable of assisting me. The room was in a great mess. In the course of piling everything into suitcases and cardboard boxes, I came on a gaunt, coarsely stitched volume, with Hebrew lettering stamped on its cardboard covers. I was just about to throw it in the box with all his other books when Leib, seeing it in my hand, became briefly animated and coherent. It was, he told me, a volume of talmudic 'Responsa', written by his grandfather (my great-grandfather), Rabbi Zvi Yakov Oppenheim of Kelme, who had died before the book appeared in 1920.

Inside the book, for which it was obviously intended to serve as a frontispiece, yet bearing no sign of ever having been stitched in with the rest, was a photograph of the author. It showed him as he must have been towards the end of his life: a frail-looking old man with a high, bare brow, a straight-sided skullcap above

it and a long, raggedly fringed, white beard. I suspect that by
then his features must have looked almost as dim, as rubbed
out by time, as they were in this reproduction. The title of the
volume was given simply as SEFER [i.e. BOOK]; the author's
name as ZVI (GENIUS) JACOB OPPENHEIM. Below that, in turn,
was a long explanatory subtitle in the flowery Hebrew of the
time, in which the contents were described as '*Questions and
Answers, Interpretations and Explanations, in the Order of
the Talmud and Commentaries*'; and the author himself was
declared to be '*The Honoured Master and Teacher, the Great
and True Genius, the Prince of Torah, a Lion Among his
Companions, the Righteous and Everlasting Upholder of Truth,
Sometime President of the Rabbinical Court of Kelme*'.

As combined title, blurb and author's bio, it seemed hard to
beat. Leib had taken the book and translated this material for
me, which was set out in conventional Hebrew type. Every other
page was like a patchwork counterpane of juxtaposed texts,
printed in an obscure Hebrew orthography. As he fluttered
through them, Leib's manner became once again abstracted
and agitated. It was terrible stuff, he said. Worthless. Talmudic
pilpul (hair-splitting). With the lordly contempt of the modern
man and rationalist he firmly believed himself to be, even at
that moment – broken down, slippered, wearing an unbuttoned
pyjama top and the trousers of a lounge suit, his eyes concealed
behind the thumb-smeared lenses of his spectacles – he dis-
missed his grandfather's life and intellectual endeavours with a
single sentence: 'He knew nothing else, poor man.' I thought
he was going to drop the book into the box in front of
him. Instead he suddenly pressed it into my hands. 'Keep it!'
he said, with a scornful insistence that was hard to interpret. I
did not know who was the target of his contempt: myself or
our common ancestor, Zvi Yakov Oppenheim, the lion among
his companions, the righteous and everlasting upholder of truth.

'Go on!' he repeated. 'Keep it! With my compliments.'

After a moment's hesitation I decided to do so. After all, Leib had kept it with him all those years, though he claimed to despise it.

It was plain to me that only someone steeped in the same tradition of talmudic scholarship as Zvi Yakov would ever be able to make head or tail of the book. I was not a scholar of that kind; nor did I know anyone who was, all the author's grandchildren and great-grandchildren included. So after I had brought it home the book remained unopened among the other oversized volumes in my bookshelves. Only by stretching my imagination to bursting point could I conceive that other copies of it might still have been in existence in a few unguessable corners of the world. I had never heard my mother speak of it; none of my cousins, Leib's children among them, knew anything about it until I mentioned it to them. Sometimes I wondered what would become of it when I reached, as I eventually will, whatever form of incapacity finally awaits me. To whom would I pass it on? On what occasion?

Long after Leib's death I happened to go to a lecture given in London by Rachile Kostanian, the curator of the Jewish State Museum of Lithuania. She turned out to be a fine-featured, slightly built, quietly spoken woman, in command of a fluent, expressive, unidiomatic English. The room in which she spoke (not a large one) was packed; people even sat on the floor or leaned against the walls. Confining herself to the events that took place in Vilnius between June 1941 and September 1943, when the ghetto was finally liquidated, and speaking throughout in an understated, undramatic fashion, she told a tale of such horror that two of the people present were driven to leave the room. I stayed on; but when it was over I felt there was something unnatural, even uncanny, about finding myself back in the quiet Hampstead street in which I had parked my car earlier. It was early evening, in mid-spring; a lively breeze was blowing; young leaves and shredded clouds went happily about their business overhead. The sun was lower; that was the only difference from before.

Towards the end of the lecture the speaker had made a dignified, modest appeal for funding. Though the museum received some support from the government of the new Lithuanian republic, she said, it was desperately short of original materials to display, both because the Nazis had destroyed so much and because it was too poor to buy articles that might come up for sale in the West. 'Most of what we have,' she said, 'is only photocopies. Not even our photographs are original.'

Subsequently I wrote to her, giving her the dates when I would be in Vilnius and saying that I hoped to meet her then. I did not tell her that I had decided to take two items with me on my journey, with the intention of leaving them in the museum (if she should wish to accept them). One of these was itself not an 'original', but a copy of the photograph of Heshel Melamed described in an earlier chapter. The other was the book by his father-in-law and my great-grandfather, Zvi Yakov Oppenheim of Kelme.

[10]

Like many others I suffer from a recurring nightmare, and have done so ever since my childhood. Though it is peopled by different characters and is enacted in a different setting each time, the dream has always been the same, whenever and wherever I have dreamt it.

Initially the place and people which figure in it are dream-casual or dream-implausible – sometimes both at once – and arouse no fear. Then, for no reason I know of, a sinister alteration occurs. I cannot describe the alteration, since everything else remains just as it was before, and the other persons present simply carry on with what they are doing. They even continue talking to me, unaware of the dread-in-advance that has gripped me.

If only I had been more alert earlier! But alert to what? Alert when? That is a mystery. I am not as I was before, and I cannot avoid any of what is to follow.

Of course not. The trap has been sprung. Too late, I know it. The power of movement has gone from me. It is impossible now for me to raise my hand, turn my head, roll my eyes, open my mouth. No wonder the people around me are unconscious of what I am going through, since I have no means of signalling it to them. Ignorant, inane, preoccupied by whatever dream-business engages them, they remain as they were. I alone have been transformed. I have become an object, a thing as rigid as an iron bar.

Except that an iron bar is incapable of feeling terror and horror at its own condition.

Unspeakable attempts to liberate myself follow; paroxysms I cannot describe, since all I know afterwards is that I have been through them. Even when I begin to sense the pillows under my head and the bedclothes over me, my hands, head and legs remain locked. Only after further struggles, repeated attempts to break free, accompanied by a heavy pounding at the heart, am I allowed to go. A sense of the pointless horror of what I have been through, rather than relief, is what I finally open my eyes to.

Again! That is the thought which greets me. It is dark. I am safe. My limbs move as I wish them to.

In another version of the dream it is not the power of movement that is taken from me, but just (just!) the ability to breathe. I stagger, flail, even hurl myself against walls and floors in my attempts to draw air into my lungs. None of it helps. Once again the people around me take no notice of the convulsions that have seized me. They are not to be cut short by anything I can do.

Whatever these dreams are precipitated by – apnoeas, malfunctions of the autonomic nervous system – I do not believe they 'symbolize' anything. They are what they are: not translations or codings of experience, but experiences in themselves, mysterious and self-sufficient events.

That said, I have sometimes thought that nightmares like these perhaps bring me as close as I can ever come to the fate of blood relations I have never seen and know nothing about, other than the manner of their death. And of countless numbers like them, who died as they did. Their disbelieving eyes looked into the eyes of indifferent, distracted murderers, and met no response. They uttered cries their murderers ignored. Their knowledge of what was being done to them came only to torment them, never to save them.

PART THREE

Lithuania

[11]

My first impression of Lithuania was of its emptiness.

The further east the plane flew, the less demarcated the landscape became, the fewer were the roads crossing it, the more rarely were vehicles to be seen. Ploughed fields turned into pasture lands, pastures into woods, woods into water, water into tussocky heaths and marshes. Each change was marked by a simple, limited change of colour. No one appeared to be moving in the villages randomly dotted about. There were no mountains; hardly any hills. Dirt roads stretched between one cluster of steep-roofed habitations and the next. The plane hissed, hummed, tilted, straightened itself out with a purposeful groan, lurched lower once more. The sun was setting directly behind it. We were dropping into shadow.

The place looked almost as empty after we landed as it had from above. Quiet too, inside and outside the airport. There was no bustle of arrival. The plane had been barely a quarter full, so little time was lost in debarking or waiting for luggage in the dimly lit hall. To judge from the newspapers they had read on the flight, the other passengers were almost all Lithuanians coming home. By the time my son and I emerged from the terminal – all angled walls of glass and a plethora of tubular green banisters – they had already cleared off. No more than three or four cars and a battered, lifeless bus were still in the parking lot. Also waiting near the exit was a man holding a sign bearing the name of the hotel I had booked into. I was relieved to see him. It soon became apparent that he had no English at all; no German or French either. The only other definitely non-Lithuanian person who had been on the plane with us, a frail-looking Indian in a double-breasted suit, with the inevitable flat, hard, black, businessman's briefcase in his hand, had also evidently been expecting to be met and was now going through the painful process of learning that his hosts had let him down. He looked about him anxiously and followed our departure with envious eyes.

Close to the airport, but apparently not part of it, was a group of houses two or three storeys high, roofed with tiles, fronted in dusty reddish or lemon-coloured stucco; handsome and elaborate in appearance, though shabby too, with bits of mock-rustication, like frayed elbows, at their corners. Nobody was to be seen in them or near them. Next came some humbler, single-storeyed wooden cottages, each with a gabled protrusion in front – a place in which to shed coats and boots before entering the dwelling proper – and a window poking out of the half-attic above. Village-like in appearance, but without a shop or bar to serve them, they too seemed to be deserted. It was only about nine in the evening, in midsummer, not raining: so where were all the people?

I could not ask this question of the driver. Silenced, diffident, middle-aged, he kept his eyes on the road. Not even the sight of a fox dashing across it provoked him to utter a sound. At ground level it was easy to understand the curiously bland appearance of the country from the air. It was virtually without fences. The edges of ploughed fields, copses and meadows met and parted on equal terms, with never a sign of greeting or mutual exclusion between them. Only the gardens of the occasional houses were fenced off; and a group of smallish, multi-windowed factories standing on a cleared slope. Modest boards

outside them told us nothing we could understand. No advertisement hoarding gave a clue as to what might be manufactured
within. Bottle tops? Shoelaces? Matchsticks?

A car. Another one. At last, a couple walking. Another couple
waiting at a bus stop. The huge red ball of the sun stands proud
of the serrated tree tops on the horizon. Some blocks of flats
appear. Even they look unpeopled. Only when the road passes
through the middle of a heavily wooded cemetery within an
elaborate, miniature topography of hills, hollows and rocky
knolls do we come on anything resembling a throng. It is made
up entirely of stone and bronze figures: angels, life-size images
of Jesus carrying his cross or already mounted on it, many
Marys with heads bowed or arms held out. There are also a
few effigies of the human departed, in frock coats. The tallest
of them are lit up momentarily in random rays from the sun.
Then a few more roads come together and sidle off from one
another – and here we are, on the edge of the Old Town of
Vilnius.

The main building of the hotel was imposing enough. A veranda
and a row of fat, primrose-coloured columns looked across a
courtyard adorned with lawns, flowerbeds and, in one corner,
tables for eating and drinking. Subsequently I discovered that
the premises had once belonged to a monastery; in fact, as if
they were loath to let the place go entirely, a succession of
corpulent monks from the Russian Orthodox cathedral across
the road used to come regularly to eat there. Their floor-length
robes were black, or cherry-red, or bright green, and they wore
hats to match. They never parted from one another without a
ceremonial kissing of hands and an exchange of embraces which
brought their tummies together with a gentle bump.

Everything had so far gone like clockwork, just as the phone
calls and faxes from and to London had requested and promised.
Now we discovered that the young woman on duty at the desk

had no English, no German, no French, no Spanish (my son's contribution), and no record of our intended arrival. Nor was there anyone, her gestures proclaimed, whom she could turn to for help. All she could do was to run her hand frantically through her thick bush of blonde, ringleted hair, pick up one piece of paper after another, study it, sigh at it and let it fall back on the heap. Finally she gave us a form to sign and led us to a 'sveet' across the courtyard.

It had two rooms, all right, but only one bed. Both of us balked at this. Back to the office, more scanning and sighing, and another pilgrimage to a single room with a small skylight in lieu of a window, which my son said he would take. I was then led across the courtyard to a room with bathroom. Fine. I was about to go down and get something to eat when I noticed a pair of well-worn men's shoes under the bed I had just been given; another look around the room revealed two dark suits hanging in the wardrobe and a suitcase tucked in a corner. Back across the courtyard. Girl cannot understand what I am talking about. Girl brought over to see for herself what I mean. Back to her desk. Back yet again across the courtyard, in a procession of two, in front of me her wild head of hair and the tiny black skirt in which her bottom is constricted. Now she takes me to the 'president's sveet', which consists of no less than three rooms in a row, all oversized and underfurnished. They are carpeted throughout in a grey material as rough as coconut matting. The suite contains two bathrooms, one unusable on account of its sewerish stink, the other tolerable simply because it is so much larger, both without ventilation.

Yes, this will do.

Not the least strange part of these proceedings is that, aside from the mysterious absentee occupant of the second bedroom I had been offered, I can see and hear no sign of there being any other guests in the hotel.

*

Much the same, it seemed to me, could have been said of Vilnius as a whole. On our first outing it looked as if the city was inhabited by about fourteen people. We went up some narrow, cobbled alleyways and through irregularly sloping squares. Streetlamps with lights inside them were almost as rare as people. Admittedly it was by now approaching eleven o'clock on a Tuesday night; this first impression of vacancy was to be somewhat modified in the days that followed. Amid the darkness and general depopulation there were a few large plate-glass windows behind which one could make out displays of chairs or glassware aspiring to elegance and high modernity: to a positively Finnish finish. But most of the shops were meagrely and dirtily windowed, still under the Communist blight, as if nothing had changed since the death of the old order, or ever would.

After some wandering about we found a couple of open cafés. Our attempts to communicate with the waitress in the one of our choice were met with helpless shrugs and giggles. But the menu eventually brought to us had English alongside the Lithuanian version, and we indicated with our fingers what we wanted. I chose a glass of beer and what the menu called 'Beer Accompaniments'. These turned out to be pieces of a hard, brittle, sour cheese so unfamiliar in taste and texture it could have been made out of pig's milk or squirrel's sweat for all I could tell. The beer, on the other hand, was excellent. 'Ustena Ale' it was called. The other English words on the label read: 'Is brewed with malt, rice, hops, yeast, and pure water only'. The choice of my son, Simon, was 'roasted fish'. The smell of garlic that came from it was so strong I was relieved to think we would not be sharing a room for that night, at least.*

---

*Items offered to us from other English-language menus included: Bread salad; Rubbed chicken soup; Meat and tinned vegetables; Fried eggs with nork; Could Lithuanian (*sic*); Natural chicken leg with plumps; Boiled rise; Lithuanian beaten pork.

He ate with pleasure; but his air remained disconsolate. Fatigue, the bathos of our attempts to communicate with the three people we had so far encountered, the spooky emptiness of the streets around us, had evidently affected him. He suddenly said, 'I've never before been in a country I know so little about.'

To my own surprise, and with a feeling of relief at making the confession, I answered, 'Neither have I.'

That was exactly how I felt: family history notwithstanding. Now that I had at last arrived in Lithuania, and was sitting in a café in its capital city, eating peculiar cheese and drinking beer, my presence there felt as arbitrary to me as his obviously did to him. (He had volunteered to come with me, and I had been glad to take up the offer, knowing him to be independent in his habits and well used to coping in foreign parts with conditions much harsher physically than anything I expected to encounter.) What was the point of it? The curiosity which had led me here now seemed frail and wilful; nothing more. I could not connect anything around me with my memories of my mother or grandmother; their lives before I had known them had never seemed to me so remote and inaccessible. And as for Heshel Melamed . . .

So, as much for my sake as for Simon's, I told him in greater detail than I ever had before all I knew about my grandfather and his wife Menuchah – whom Simon had never seen. Then about the nine children produced by the two of them. Some of these great-aunts and great-uncles he had never met; two of them, it turned out, he had never heard of before. My account of the Oppenheim family in Kelme was also news to him. This led him to ask when the Jews had arrived in Lithuania (some time in the fourteenth century, not long after the Lithuanian tribes had been united by their first king, Gediminas); and from where they had come (either from Germany or south Russia, or both, depending on which historian one chose to believe); and why they had come (at the invitation of successive kings and grand dukes, who had wanted to use their skills as merchants and scribes in order to build a state out of a semi-wilderness). And what had Lithuania become afterwards? A part of Russia? A 'dual monarchy' with Poland? A part of Prussia? Yes, all of these; while remaining stubbornly itself throughout, in language and in the minds of its native people. And the Jews too had stuck it out, intermittent pogroms and the mass migrations of the late nineteenth and early twentieth centuries notwithstanding. When the Second World War began with Hitler's invasion of Poland in 1939, almost a quarter of the population of Vilnius was Jewish. Within weeks that proportion was greatly increased by the thousands of refugees who had fled eastwards from Poland after the German *blitzkrieg* on that country. The 'lucky' ones among them were deported to Siberia during the subsequent, brief Russian occupation of the city; a few managed to flee with the hastily retreating Russian army; the rest were trapped when the Germans arrived. Of these, all but a handful were dead by the end of the war.

A strange thought suddenly occurred to me. No wonder the city appeared to be so empty! A quarter – no, a third eventually – of the people who had once lived here had been wiped out. All around us were the spaces they had occupied. We were in the midst of a vacancy their absence had created; the city's silence was that of the words they and their unborn children would never speak.

When I said something of this sort to my son, he was properly sceptical about it: not about the facts I had given him, but about my notion that their effects could be visible still and audible too, even if only by way of absence and dumbness. So long a time had passed since then; the population of the whole of Europe, and of its capital cities especially, had grown greatly during the past decades; many more people were bound to be living in Vilnius today than when the war had ended, fifty years before. They were just a very quiet lot, that was all. They didn't stay out late. Not on a Tuesday night. Not in this part of town, anyway.

It was impossible to argue the point. Yet what I had said was one of those thoughts which, once uttered, is not to be unthought. It was with me still as we walked back to the hotel, via a different set of romantically ill-lit, decrepit alleyways. (One of them, I noticed, went by the name of Literaturi, as if to show me what a civilized country we were visiting.) All were as silent as before.

The next morning I set out for the Jewish Museum. This involved walking through the Old Town once again. It was more extensive than I had thought it to be the previous evening, and more richly endowed with handsome yet unpretentious old buildings in diverse styles: Baltic Baroque, Nordic Neo-classical; Poor Man's St Petersburg. (The last consisting of shabby courtyards faced in broken stucco, with flat-topped carriage entrances from the street.)

The allure of Europe! Of old Europe, anyway! Still with me, as ever. I had succumbed to it the moment I set foot on the continent for the first time, at the age of twenty-one. And always, even then, as an infatuated colonial newcomer, the sense of black betrayal at the heart of it all. Some of the low, charmingly crooked streets I was walking through, now care-fully preserved and presented to visitors as 'heritage' Vilnius, had in fact been part of the city's Jewish quarter, which the Germans had transformed into a patrolled, fenced-off ghetto: a place of slavery, 'selections', 'actions' and a final 'liquidation' in September 1943.

All done with now. History. Behold, Rabbi Heshel Melamed, your grandson walking the streets, admiring the architecture. In perfect safety too.

Many of the public buildings, even the most dignified of

them, had a pleasingly modest look, appropriate to a provincial capital. That is not how I would describe the biggest of the churches, however. Later, from the battlements of an ancient, brick-built fort on the bank of the Neris River, I was to count no less than thirteen basilica-like structures dominating the skyline of the Old Town and the areas immediately around it. Their black and grey domes strained against the sky like balloons; their gilded crosses heliographed important messages to one another whenever the sun allowed. Most were Catholic (of the Lithuanian or Polish varieties), two or three Orthodox Russian, one Lutheran. Some had monasteries attached, some not. Below domes and crosses their portly bodies were decked out in cream and yellow; stalk-like clusters of pillars supported smaller domes at every available vantage point. Collectively they resembled a gathering of overweight officials, with necks bulging over the back of their collars, confident that their services will always be in demand.

The Jewish Museum cut a figure of quite a different kind. More or less concealed by a rundown block of apartments, with an empty space in front of it and some shade-giving trees hanging over it, it looked like an enlarged version of the wooden cottages I had seen near the airport, and was to see again all over the Lithuanian countryside. Narrow shingles, painted green; steep wooden roof; a dormer window or two squeezed into whatever space was available above – all these, without ever losing their unfamiliarity, always struck my eye with a puzzling intimacy. Perhaps it was because of their surprising likeness, despite the different materials used in their construction, to the low, iron-roofed houses in South Africa in which so many of the immigrants had made their first homes. The museum even had a narrow wooden *stoep* in front of it. When walked on, it made a noise I could recall from my childhood.

Though I understood why Rachile Kostanian was pleased at the prospect, I could not help feeling some regret when I learned from her that the museum would soon be leaving these premises and moving into a larger, permanent building about to be made available by the state authorities.

The handing over to Rachile of my grandfather's photograph, of my great-grandfather's BOOK, and the accompanying loose-leaf picture of him, together with a few notes of explanation about each of these items, was hardly a ceremonious occasion. Chaotic would probably be a better word for it. For this she could not be blamed. We met in her office just after she had finished showing a small group of Germans around the museum and just before she was about to take the same party to visit the site of the former ghetto. So she was under pressure anyway. No sooner had we begun our conversation than we were interrupted by a plump, dark-chinned young man in a suit of Lithuanian cut (plenty of spare cloth; lethally pointed lapels) who had come to meet the Germans and who, I gathered, was an important personage in the country's tiny, reconstituted Jewish community. So Rachile went out, introduced him to the waiting Germans and came back into the office. She had just sat down again when the door was pushed open by a bespectacled, thirtyish American in his shirt sleeves. A black-muzzled camera, ready for action, dangled down his chest; a canvas bag secured by enough straps and buckles to get him up Mont Blanc hung from his back; an open map was clutched in his hand. Accoutrements swinging fore and aft, he advanced to the desk, interrupted us in mid-sentence and would not leave or fall silent until Rachile had explained to him, in detail, where at Paneriai was the memorial to the thousands of Jews who had been massacred there, and where he would find another memorial on which – he had heard – his grandfather's name appeared.

Why he was so convinced that his business with his grandfather took precedence over my business with my grandfather I do not know, and could not ask him without initiating a row of some kind between us. The thought of competing with him, in these circumstances, for Rachile's exhausted attention was grotesque: to me, anyway, if not to him. She appeared to be under greater strain here than when she had been in London, perhaps because of the effort she had just made with the group waiting for her return, and the further effort with them that lay ahead. Her eyes looked darker than I had remembered; her delicate hand shook slightly as she wrote out instructions for the American; she seemed to have difficulty in drawing breath between each utterance.

When he had left she sat silently for a moment. I was conscious of the faint rise and fall of her shoulders inside the fawn, librarian-type blouse she was wearing, with its sleeves buttoned at the wrists and a small bow at the neck. She put a hand to her temple and said, 'Sometimes when it's so busy I can't sleep in the night. Today would be a good day for me to stay at home. But you know – when there are Germans coming – it's always specially important that I speak to the Germans.'

On first coming into the museum I had actually chosen – partly out of curiosity, partly because the rooms were so small – to join the group already there: i.e. the Germans. Exhausted and indefatigable, shaky and dedicated, Rachile took them around, speaking in English, while a man who, I guess, was a member of the group rather than a guide translated into German what she said. He kept his voice low; those in the party who occasionally asked questions of Rachile through their translator spoke in whispers only, their faces strained into immobility throughout. Only their eyes moved, flickering across the terrible pictures on display in several of the rooms, and then gazing down at the floor again. It was impossible not to feel sorry for them, not to admire them even; after all, they had volunteered for this visit, they had not been compelled to make it. Most of them were jacketless; it was a hot June day outside, though within the wooden walls of the museum, under the shade of the trees, the air was cool. They numbered about a half-dozen, men and women, young to middle-aged. All were middle class in appearance.

Whatever sins of commission or omission their parents or grandparents might have been accused of, they were wholly free of blame, they carried no responsibility for what had been done in the name of their people. While explaining one of the many ancient, ill-reproduced, enlarged snapshots of atrocity hanging on the walls – adults and children being marched away in long lines; stripped of their clothes; fallen into trenches and ditches or turned into charred shapes lying in burned-out synagogues; all accompanied by the men who were about to do or had just done the shooting and burning, most of them in German uniform, some (Lithuanian militiamen) in civilian clothes decorated with white armbands, to show how important and 'official' was the business they were on – while Rachile was explaining such a picture, she said, 'And then the Germans gave the order – ' promptly caught herself up and said, 'You must excuse me – I should say, then the *Nazis* gave the order . . .' and continued with her tale. One or two members of the group, with enough English to pick up the correction, quickly shook their heads: as if to indicate, I thought, that they understood the courtesy she was extending to them, but did not wish her to apologize to them for anything she had to say.

Another room, in which no horrors were to be seen, only pictures of perfectly commonplace-looking Lithuanian men and women, Rachile described with great emphasis as '*for us* – a very important room'. Few in number, the pictures were of gentiles of all classes and conditions who had risked their lives by sheltering and preserving Jews from the killers hunting them. Alongside some of the pictures were photocopied certificates from the Yad Vashem Holocaust Memorial in Jerusalem, commemorating them as Righteous Gentiles. Among them was a portrait of the mother of Vytautis Landsbergis, the first President of the independent, post-Soviet Lithuanian republic. The group studied the portraits attentively; but asked no questions.

The tour was over. The visitors queued up to sign the book in the little hall. One of the women wiped her eyes and blew her nose. On a subsequent, solitary visit to the museum I had a look at what they had written. Their sentiments were predictable but appeared no less heartfelt for being so. 'Never again,' they wrote. 'We have seen things here to shame us.' 'We must never forget.' And so forth.

[12]

Those were the circumstances, then, in which a copy of Heshel Melamed's portrait and the last existing copy of Zvi Yakov's posthumous BOOK were handed over to the Jewish Museum. I did not see Rachile on my next visit there, which was made many days later, though we spoke again on the telephone before I left Vilnius and have exchanged letters since my return to London. In the last letter I had from her she mentioned that the BOOK would be displayed at an exhibition to be mounted during the forthcoming bicentenary of the death of Rabbi Elijah, the Vilna Gaon, the most famous of all Lithuanian rabbis. The celebrations are being sponsored by various interested bodies abroad, in Israel and the United States in particular, and by the Lithuanian government.

Not surprisingly, there is a portrait of the Vilna Gaon in the first room one comes to in the museum. It might be called the only happy room in the place, for it celebrates with whatever materials are available all aspects of Jewish life in the country, before that life came to its end. There are photographs of eminent rabbis and of the title-pages of books written by them, of religious incunabula long since lost, of now-destroyed synagogues and talmudic schools. On another wall are photographs of a different kind: they show newspapers and political proclamations, earnest Zionist or Bundist (Jewish socialist)

conferences and conventions, Jewish members of the independent Lithuanian parliament in the inter-war years,
Lithuanian Jews who had won fame abroad (Chaim Soutine,
the painter, prominent among them). Yiddish poets too, some
of whose poems I had read in translation many years before.
To my mind, the most heartbreaking of these pictures was a
big group photograph of the young men and women who had
attended the 'Maccabiad' meeting organized by the Maccabi
Athletic Association in Vilnius, in the summer of 1936. Hundreds of smiling youngsters appear in it, runners and swimmers,
hurdlers and boxers, the men in white athletic vests, the women
in white blouses.

Exactly five years to go.

It was there, in that happy room as I have called it, that I
began to realize how little reconstructed since my childhood
had been my view of 'the old country' and the neighbouring
countries like it. The rabbinical books shown on the walls
meant nothing to me, and I could feel no retrospective sense of
loss that my education had not equipped me to read them; the
names of most of the rabbis pictured alongside were unknown
to me, and I had no hankering to have studied or prayed with
any of them. But so what? None of them would have had much
use for me either. Nor would most of my own forebears have
cared for my company, in all probability, though they might
have mourned to see what my upbringing had made of me and
what I have made of myself. The men pictured on these walls
(only men were pictured in the 'religious section' of the room)
had had their own lives to live. They had devoted themselves to
their faith and to the modes of learning derived from it; a
companionship with predecessors they hoped to emulate had
enriched their lives; they had admired and competed against
their contemporaries. Naturally they had suffered too: from
illness, financial worries, fear of anti-Semitic bandits and officials, marital unhappiness, self-doubt, bereavements. They had

also been divided into a variety of sects and factions which often spoke ill of each other and conspired against one another; there were even cases of them informing against one another to the Russian authorities. Again: so what? Their sense of their own worth and importance was not to be wrested from them, neither then nor now, not by their gentile neighbours, not by their opponents within the Jewish community and not by Zvi Yakov's ignorant great-grandson either.

That on one side; and on the other the various forms of secular striving and ambition mentioned above; and, as I was soon to see outside the museum, on one Vilnius's busiest roads, an imposing building which had once housed the only Yiddish-medium technical high school in the world. (Even the textbooks used there had been printed in Yiddish.) Later still, in Kaunas, I was to visit the house in which an obsessed, late-nineteenth-century Jewish *luftmensch* and internationalist by the name of Zamenhof had invented Esperanto; and to stand on the terrace overlooking the Neris River where yet another *luftmensch* by the name of Mapu, the single-handed inventor of the novel in modern Hebrew, used to seat himself and wait for inspiration to come.

All this in Lithuania, that Nowhere of a place, that desolate Pale of prayer, pogroms and deprivation?

Still, it all ended as we know it did.

I had not known before this visit – or if I had read it somewhere I had put it out of mind – the full extent of the devastation wreaked on the Jewish communities of Lithuania and Latvia during the war. Only 5 per cent of the Jews living there at the time of the German invasion were alive four years later.

That is to say: one in twenty survived.

Nor had I known – or if I had known I had chosen not to remember it – the speed with which these communities were wiped out. The Germans invaded Lithuania on 22 June 1941.

By the end of August the 'overwhelming majority of the Jews in the provinces [had been] slaughtered . . . From September to November, most of the Jews in the large cities, who had been interned in the ghettos, were liquidated in similar fashion.'

That is to say: in towns and villages scattered all over Lithuania, a country roughly the size of Ireland, 600 years of Jewish life were brought to an end over a period of ten weeks only.

Rifle and machine-gun fire was the method of 'liquidation' referred to, together with some mass burnings of those locked into hospitals and synagogues. By the beginning of December 1941 SS Standardführer Karl Jaeger, head of *Einsatzkommando* 3, was able to boast to his superiors that only 15 per cent of Lithuanian Jewry (all of them what he called 'work Jews'; most of them in the ghettos of Kaunas and Vilnius) were still alive. 'I can confirm today that *Einsatzkommando* 3,' he wrote, 'has reached the goal of solving the Jewish problem in Lithuania.'

As if the task of 'solving the Jewish problem in Lithuania' was not achievement enough for him, his victims by that date also included thousands of men, women and children from Germany (from Berlin, Munich, Vienna and elsewhere) who had been dragged to Kaunas, confined under atrocious conditions for several days and then shot. Such feats of annihilation were recorded by Jaeger and others like him all over eastern Europe well before the first gas chambers were put into operation in Chelmno; the report quoted above predates by a full three months the initial use of gas in Auschwitz. The methods of mass murder used by Jaeger's unit and all the other *Einsatzkommandos* and their Lithuanian auxiliaries were at no time abandoned in the years ahead; only complemented by others more 'efficient'.

In one of the rooms in the Vilnius museum there is an enlarged photocopy of an official summary by Karl Jaeger of his activities in Lithuania over one particular period. Many names I had heard in conversations among Jewish contemporaries at home – always pronounced as if they were a sort of private joke – 'Oh, my grandparents came from a little place in Lithuania called "Mariampole", or "Panevzys", or "Ariogala"' – appear to desolating effect in the list, along with countless others unfamiliar to me. The document has a handwritten, boxed superscription in ink above it: *Geheime Reichsache!* (Secret State Matters!). Everything else is neatly typed and presented with a doubtless bogus but nevertheless deadly exactitude: Jaeger, as commanding officer of the unit, showing himself to be a zealous servant, a punctilious worker, a proud and devoted SS officer doing exactly what is expected of him.

There is a photograph of him too, in his tunic and helmet, the former hung about with no less than two Iron Crosses, for heroism. He is fat-faced, self-assured, self-impressed. Not in his wildest, most ambitious fantasies can he have imagined the scale of his success: that he would grow up to be a pitiless god, a mass murderer, the head killer of an entire country's Jews. He has *done* it; he has become the biggest thing on the horizon for hundreds of miles around.

So there is Jaeger's summary, and there are the names of the towns: Kaunas, Jonava, Trakai, Babtai, and scores of others. In columns, like this:

Rasenai	5.8.41	213 Jews	66 Jewish women
Rasenai (district)	18.8.41	466 Jews	440 Jewish women
			1,020 Jewish children
Rasenai	16.9.41	294 Jews	
Rasenai	29.9.41	254 Jews	1 Lithuanian communist

These references to Rasenai I copied down during my second, solitary visit to the museum. By then I had spent a few more days in Vilnius and longer still in other parts of Lithuania. The

name Rasenai stood out for me not just because it recurred so
often on the list (so did others, some with considerably larger
totals alongside) but because in the meantime I had been to
Rasenai and had acquired my own vivid impressions of the
place – not knowing, of course, that I would so soon see repeated
references to it in this room, in a photocopy of a page from this
kind of ledger. But that was not the only reason why its repeated
appearance on the list struck me with particular force. Rasenai
was (for all I know it still is) the district 'capital' for Varniai
and all the towns and villages for a considerable distance around
it. It was the place where Heshel Melamed went in 1908, to get
the Russian identity document which is still in my possession.
It was as someone born and resident in 'Rasenai ap.' that my
mother is described on the Lithuanian passport which carried
her to safety in South Africa.

That was my grandfather's Rasenai and hers. And mine? We
had gone to Rasenai merely because our guide claimed that a
restaurant on its outskirts was famous for serving the best
known of all Lithuanian national dishes. As we arrived there
earlier than had been planned, he suggested that we spend some
time in the town itself before driving on to the restaurant. Which
we did.

It was noon, on a Saturday, and not a lot was happening.
Several elderly people were sitting on benches in the sunshine
or shade of its central square. The bleak, oversized, Soviet-era
buildings around the square – a post office big enough for a
town hall; shops with plenty of grime on their windows and
nothing for sale on their shelves – were already closed. To one
side was a sculpture of a young Lithuanian hero, more than life-
size, striding forward against fate and all Lithuania's enemies:
Poles, Germans, Russians and in all probability Jews too. His
attire consisted of loose shirt, floppy trousers, long coat and
bristling moustache. A faintly tumescent girdle hung below his
waist and sprang forward between his legs. All these were made

of white stone. His chin was lowered, indicating not depression but stubbornness. One arm was outstretched in front of him, the other clutched an item which might have been a cudgel, or a bunch of flowers, or a defunct lion à la Hercules. His name was Amzias Budeiau. (At least I think it was his name.)

Then I noticed a large number of policemen standing about on the far side of the square. So I walked over to see what they were doing. Before I could get across the howl of a siren abruptly split the air. The men sprang to attention. Children came running. In the same instant a fleet of what looked like runaway rickshaws or perambulators emerged into the open space. My bewilderment gave way – slowly, it seemed – to the understanding that I was watching a race by a group of disabled male athletes. There must have been twenty of them. With a whirr, a flash, a fleeting image of bowed, huddled effort, they scudded down the road, fiercely plying the wheels of their chairs. It took them no more than a minute to go by. The road was empty again. The children were no longer waving their arms. The noise of the siren receded.

We got back into the car and went on to the restaurant: an iron-roofed shack with torn curtains, on the side of a dirt road. It was closed. But we did not escape the famous Lithuanian national dish. A woman brought it to us at another place a few miles further on. It consisted of innumerable tiny balls of a greasy, mealy substance with a faint sprinkling of bacon-rind shavings on top. In the middle of each ball was a dark germ of nameless matter which looked as if it might grow, if it were planted.

That was Rasenai. For me.

I return to the second visit I paid to the Vilnius Jewish State Museum, the day before I left Lithuania, when I copied into my notebook that small extract from Jaeger's endless list. Two other things which happened during the visit remain to be recorded, if only because of the unexpected connection between them.

I do not know how this connection is to be understood. It happened in my presence, simply. So I shall put it down.

The first 'happening' was merely a thought that had never struck me before; not with such directness anyway. Many of the photographs on the walls showed scenes of unspeakable horror. It was impossible therefore not to become aware that elements of involuntary or unacknowledged voyeurism might be involved in looking at them; or even in the prior act of feeling obliged to do so. Thinking of this, and wondering, for example, how dedicated anti-Semites and other psychopathic types might respond to the bestialities displayed in the museum, I suddenly realized that the worst of the pictures *had been taken by the killers themselves*. Or if not by the men who were actually firing the rifles and machine guns at any one moment, then certainly by their companions and accomplices.

No correspondent, neutral or otherwise, was present at any of the *Einsatz* actions in order to expose to the public 'outside' the atrocities being committed. On the contrary. Because they were afraid of the reaction from abroad if their deeds became known, the German authorities did their best to prevent word of the massacres spreading outside official circles. (They failed, of course; but they made the attempt.) They also had misgivings about the effect that treating the slaughters as a spectator sport would have on the troops who were not actually participating in the actions. (It was not mutiny and moral outrage on the soldiers' part that they feared; with unsurpassable impudence, with the naked intention of presenting themselves to themselves as the benefactors of mankind, they spoke instead of the need to preserve '*decency and discipline*' on such occasions.) Also they wanted to keep other Jews, especially those in western Europe, ignorant of the fate awaiting them, in order to make the task of 'relocating' and killing them so much easier, when their turn came. The whole activity was intended, at least until it was all over, to remain a solemn secret, as Jaeger well knew when he inscribed *Geheime Reichsache!* on the document quoted above.

The assembling of images of war and natural calamity for display on television and in the press is always a morally ambiguous business, as many war correspondents have themselves acknowledged; so is our participation as viewers and readers in the results. But this – ! Sadistic prurience was not a 'temptation' or a 'danger' for the photographers of the scenes on show here: it was precisely what had animated them. For some of the killers the taking of snapshots had served as a deferred means of gloating over their victims' torments; it kept in prospect a renewal of the fun later, when such trophies could be hauled out for inspection by the photographers and their friends.

But if that was the case, should their handiwork be put on display? Should we give them the satisfaction of tormenting their victims anew – and for ever – each time a visitor came into this museum, or any other like it?

As it happened, I had the museum to myself that morning. A grey-haired lady, whom I had met in Rachile's office the last time I was there, had opened the door to me and then returned to her office. From time to time, through its half-open door, I heard her speaking on the telephone in Lithuanian and Yiddish. Rachile herself I already knew to be out of town that day. So, pencil and notebook in hand, I was left alone. It was very quiet.

Then the doorbell rang. A party of five people came in. Four of them were tourists; the fifth was a stocky, bearded young man in what looked almost like a uniform: soft boots, khaki trousers, open-neck khaki shirt with buttoned epaulettes and clip-on pencils bristling from its breast pocket, no jacket. Of the tourists three were women; one of them old, two in early middle age. As they came into the first room, the youngest woman exclaimed joyfully, in a South African accent, 'Ah! Air-conditioning! At last!'

She was wrong. The cramped, coffin-like wooden hut was cool under its sheltering trees; but it was no more equipped with air-conditioning than with a jacuzzi or games room. In a low voice the guide began explaining to the party the history of the museum and the purpose for which it had been established. I was standing in the room beyond. While the guide was addressing them, the male tourist detached himself from the others and approached me through the open doorway. 'Excuse me asking,' he said, 'are you from America?' 'No,' I answered, 'from England.' 'Well,' he informed me, 'we're from South Africa.' 'I can hear that,' I replied. This provoked from him the answer it probably deserved: 'To me you sound a bit like a South African too.' 'Yes. I've been living in England for many years.' Struck by this, he went back to the women. 'That gentleman's from South Africa too!' he said, interrupting the guide. Exclamations of interest followed. Now it was the turn of one of the women. Dressed in beige linen trousers and jacket, with dark brown blouse, handbag and shoes by way of contrast, she came over and asked, 'Where you from then?' 'Kimberley.' 'Really?' She pondered this answer for a few moments. 'No,' she had to admit finally, with some disappointment, 'I don't think I know anybody from Kimberley. We're from Joh'burg.'

They did not linger in any of the rooms, and no further contact was made between us until I was joined by the old woman. Broadly built, grey-haired, with heavy shoulders and a heavy tread, she too was smartly turned out, in a black and white dress. A necklace of white beads hung down well below her bosom; there were several rings on her fingers. She had a large, powdered face which wore a perpetual, short-sighted frown. She did not speak to me, but craned her head forward to look at the pictures. Eventually, just three or four feet away from me, she fixed her gaze on a photograph of a ghetto scene. It presented a view of commonplace misery and helplessness on one side, and of power on the other: people in rags, children in a gutter, a group of helmeted, belted, booted German soldiers with guns in their hands or slung over their shoulders. It was impossible to guess what had been happening the moment before the picture was taken, or what was going to happen the moment after.

'You see that picture?' she said to me, drawing her head back and pointing at it. I recognized her accent as promptly as I had the younger people's. She was a native Yiddish-speaker; and not just any kind of Yiddish-speaker either, but a Litvak. She spoke firmly, hoarsely, doggedly almost, but without any special emphasis: it was clear that she simply felt compelled, because I was there, because I was a stranger and we had met in this place, to tell me something. 'That's just what it was. You see it? I was here in the war. I was in Kovno Ghetto. Afterwards they sent me to Auschwitz. When the war ended I went to my family in Cape Town.'

Then she did a strange thing. It would have seemed strange to me anyway, even if I had not been alone in the silent museum for so long beforehand, and not been thinking as I had about the origin of many of the pictures on the walls. She reached into her handbag and took out a small camera. With some difficulty she unbuttoned the flaps that covered the lens and bent her knees in order to level it, from a distance of inches only, at the sad, blurry photograph she had been studying. Her open handbag hung by its strap from the crook of her arm. She pressed the button on the camera; a click and convulsive whine followed. She lowered the camera and looked unhappily at it. Again she brought it to her eyes and pressed the button. Another click, another whine.

'What is the good of that?' she asked, with genuine distress. 'Why doesn't the flash flash?'

I could not help her. I did not know what to say.

The man I had spoken to earlier (her son? her nephew?) called from the entrance hall. She gave the camera a severe shake, shrugged, nodded at me and returned it to her handbag. Her footsteps retreated heavily. The front door closed behind the group. Then it opened again. The guide returned. He was alone and came straight to me. We had not exchanged a word previously. In formal, gentlemanly fashion, yet also somewhat strangely, I thought, he said, 'You must excuse us for disturbing you, sir. But it is my work.'

[13]

There were several different kinds of Vilnius, I discovered; Old Town Vilnius, with its small-scale grandeurs and decrepitudes, was just one them. There was the downtown, commercial Vilnius of Gediminas Street, lined with the nearest thing the city had to department stores, smart restaurants and boutiques; on it also stood a four-square structure, flanked by trees and a kind of miniature mall, which had served the Soviet occupiers as their local Lubyanka. The building was now marked by a memorial to the Lithuanians who had been held inside it, interrogated and sentenced to death either immediately or (more lingeringly) in the Gulag. The street itself ended on Cathedral Square, where an old woman stood next to a set of scales even older than she was. Passers-by who wanted to know their weight would hand her a few aluminium coins of a barely conceivable worthlessness and she would do the rest. Business was not brisk, but she was patient. At the end of the day she wrapped her weights in a cloth bag and shackled them, along with her scales, to a nearby tree. Ready for the next day.

Some yards from her pitch was deadbeat Vilnius, where male and female drunks lay about on benches. One of them, a man with a bad limp, a roll-up stuck perpetually in the corner of his mouth, and sunglasses dangling from a single shaft, wore on his chest a weighty, hand-carved, wooden crucifix, complete

134

with Jesus. He would hold it out whenever he caught your eye: in admonition, I thought, rather than an appeal for funds. An equally pious female companion had a practice of bringing the traffic to a screeching, cursing halt by taking up a position in the middle of Gediminas Street, in order to cross herself elaborately and say her prayers.

Further off, on the other side of the Neris River, was dormitory Vilnius, where tall apartment blocks stood in uniform rows. Between them and the river was exposition Vilnius, complete with concert hall, skating rink and football stadium. It also contained a mysterious building adorned in front by an oversized, Cretan-type female figure, several storeys high, brandishing a torch in one hand and a pair of snakes in the other. (They looked like snakes, anyway.) The national museum and the ruins of the medieval castle were nearby too, as well as Kalnu Park, one of the city's biggest. Its attractions (*atracckìony*) included tennis, skateboarding, go-karting, a merry-go-round and a bouncy castle. Also many trees – ash, sycamore, false acacia mottled with the white, sticky patches of its flowers – set out in formal rows, and a shallow but steep-banked stream, where boys fished and swam. Flat, round rocks, like oversized sucking sweets, lay under the clear water. Crows of a kind new to me, wearing grey clerical collars and black skullcaps, bounced about on the grass.

In the park I saw a Chinese lady with a child of mixed parentage: the only 'non-whites' I encountered during my stay in the country, aside from our Indian fellow passenger at the airport. In general the appearance of the Lithuanians came as a surprise to me. I had endowed them in advance with wide haunches, thick necks, broad noses and cheekbones. Instead the prevailing physical type was tall, slender, light-haired; the prevailing face obliquely refined in bone structure and expression. They looked more like Scandinavians than Slavs, yet they were not that either. Singular: like their language.

*

Behind one of the biggest of the Orthodox churches, but cut off from it by a streamlet flowing noisily towards the Neris, I found myself one morning in a neighbourhood which I first thought of as Russian or Dostoevskyan Vilnius; then as Bohemian Vilnius; and finally as a fragment of ex-Jewish Vilnius. It struck me as Russian not just because of the looming view of the Orthodox church on one side, but because it consisted of a collection of shabby, unpaved courtyards, some with carriage entrances facing directly on the road, some closed off by impenetrable heaps of rubble, some leading in semi-secretive fashion in and out of one another. Around each courtyard were tumble-down buildings, their doors and windows set in ornate but crumbling stucco frames of appropriately Muscovite colours: half-hearted yellows, vanishing pinks, pitted blues, chocolate-and-dust.

Wandering about, I came on a footpath running between the stream and a long, windowless wall. Half-way down the path I was confronted by a piece of statuary carved out of white marble. A seated female figure, about half life-size, it was parked under a tree. It had its back to the wall, its face looking towards the water, its hands in its lap. Hooded and cloaked, with something like a nun's wimple over its brow, the figure was tensed forward, as if in anxiety or concentration. It might have been a madonna (sans baby) or part of a *pietà* (sans deposition), but the features of the face and its expression were too blind and blade-like for either. It was an impressive piece of work. The longer I looked at it the more unnervingly it reminded me of a super-heroine from an American comic, or a space-person from a video game.

There it stood, or sat, anyway, half in the shade and half out of it: unattended, unexplained, contextless. When I came to the end of the wall I turned and found myself in the opening to another pair of interconnected, irregularly shaped courtyards. Some of the buildings around them were lived in; others had been roofless for so long that grass and weeds grew out of their vacant window holes, like hair from the ears of an old man. Clothes lines sagged from poles; attempts at vegetable gardens were scratched into the sand here and there; a few lime trees rose above the highest of the roofs; old cars were parked at any angle convenient for their drivers. Also scattered about the biggest of the courtyards were pieces of stone and wooden sculpture, as well as earthenware pots and jars of various sizes. The most striking item was a 'construction' rather than a sculpture: it consisted of a line of boulders running from a corner of the yard towards a hillock, which it then ascended in spiral fashion, the boulders diminishing in size the higher they went. From the hillock's centre a flat strip of iron, painted red, like an elongated flange, rose vertically to a height of about twenty feet, its end twisted into yet another spiral, as if to mime the course of stones that had led the eye to it. Guy wires lashed to spikes in the ground helped to hold the whole thing upright.

The only people to be seen were a couple sitting on a bench and a little boy playing in the open doorway of a shed nearby. The man was smoking a pipe; the woman drinking tea or coffee from a mug. It turned out that the man – bearded, thick-set, eyeing me in ill-disposed fashion – spoke Lithuanian only; but the woman confessed to having 'small English'. She had risen to her feet at my approach, putting her mug down on the bench. The man sat where he was, legs stretched out in front of him. 'What is this place?' I asked, with a gesture around me. 'It is where the artists live,' she answered simply. She looked at me with a curiosity as candid as my own. Her eyes were dark brown, like her hair; her lips were dry; she had a faintly freckled complexion; her blue, sleeveless dress was belted at the waist and had a full skirt below.

'Can I look around?' I asked.

'Of course, if you want to.'

I walked over to the construction of stones and metal and

stood at its foot, looking up. She followed me there, curious still, and perhaps wanting to practise her English. There was nothing suspicious or hostile in her manner; on the contrary, it was gentle, almost musing. Standing there, I learned that the seated man was her husband; that he was the sculptor of the female figure I had seen next to the stream; that the little boy was theirs; that she used to do printing, but was now looking after her son; that many other artists lived in these buildings. The pieces scattered about were samples of their work; so was the tall construction we were standing under. 'Also students from the art school live there,' she said, pointing to a single-storeyed building which stood on a rise by itself, to one side. There was something almost fortress-like about its appearance and the site it occupied. The naked, unpainted, unplastered state of its stone walls also distinguished it from the rest, with their coatings of crumbling stucco. One half of its roof was in a good state of repair, the rest derelict. Ragged curtains and other signs of domesticity could be seen in some of the windows, under the cared-for section of the roof; the windows further away were just empty spaces, dark within.

Now it was her turn to ask questions of me. Was I also an artist? No. A businessman? No. From America? No. England? Yes. 'So why do you come to Vilnius?' I was a tourist, I said. Her wonder grew. 'A *tourist*? You come to *Vilnius* to make a tour?' So I told her that I had come because my mother had been born in the country. She smiled, relieved to be given so simple an answer to the puzzle of my presence. 'Oh, you have family to visit here.' No, I said, I did not. The members of my mother's family who had remained in Lithuania had been killed during the war. They were Jews.

She stood silently for a moment, her wide brown eyes looking into mine. 'Now you say that,' she said artlessly, 'I see there is something Judisch – ' and she brought up her hand and moved it in circular fashion before her face. Then she pointed again at the half-ruined stone structure she had drawn my attention to before, the one where the students lived. 'You see that building? Before the war it was a Judisch synagogue.'

I turned to look at it. As if it had jumped into focus I realized that it was not only the nakedness of its walls and the relatively lofty position it occupied that set it apart from the others. I saw now that there were arches of oriental aspect above its windows – those with glass, where the students lived, and those without, where nobody lived. Like the simple pillars on which they pretended to stand, these arches were made of the same material as the rest; it was only the size and cut of the stones that delineated them. At the end of the building, above some clumsy brick infilling and a small, battered, wooden door, there rose a taller arch. I said, and heard only after I had begun that I was repeating the words she had just used about me, 'Now that you say it, I can see it.'

I do not know if she noticed the repetition. Smiling faintly, with the air of naive curiosity and concern she had shown throughout, she raised her hand towards the building again. 'Oh, everybody knows about it.'

On one of the windowsills I saw a chunk of dark wood carved into a portentous, arty shape; on another, a row of books, each with its compressed pages end-on to the window, so that their spines faced inwards; on yet another, a pot with a small green plant in it, and alongside it a pair of trainers, as if placed there for Duchamp-like effect. Bits of curtain hung down, vague shapes of furniture loomed behind, suggesting the student lives that went on within.

'The people living there – do they know it too?' I asked.

She shrugged briefly, as guileless as she was guiltless: 'Of course.'

For a moment, standing next to this tall, handsome, soft-spoken woman, the sunlight gleaming on the wave of her dark brown hair, and right inside that wave too, I felt something horribly like a sense of relief. Let the students get on with it: daubing their canvases, gouging bits of wood in whatever style they fancied, chiselling stones, turning clay into pots of all shapes. No more Hebrew prayers to be said here; no more people to say them; no rabbis like my grandfather to lead them as they did it. Nothing. One day, should an 'economic miracle' happen to Lithuania, as everyone was hoping it would, the whole area would be redeveloped, the buildings pulled down, the stones reused.

We walked back to where I had come in. I had thought of asking her to tell her husband how much the piece of sculpture outside had impressed me. He was still sitting on the bench: still growing his beard, smoking his pipe, practising his scowl. So I decided he could do without my compliments. Seeing him again I realized also that he was at least twenty years older than his wife. No doubt she had had a predecessor or two. She accompanied me as far as the path next to the stream. There she halted and put out her hand. 'My name is Maria,' she said by way of belated self-introduction. I responded by giving her my name. As we shook hands she asked if I was coming back. 'To Vilnius?' 'No – I mean here, to this place.' Ingenuous as ever, she added, 'The artists like to show their work. Maybe to sell it sometimes.'

Everything passes and is forgotten. That is the one bleak face shown to us by history.

What happens, happens for ever. That is history's other, Janus face.

We look first at the one, then at the other, over and over again. Neither offers any solace for suffering undergone.

The strongest emotions I remember from my visit to Lithuania are sadness, a stunned sadness of a kind I had never felt before, and an almost constant sense of humiliation. How feeble my imagination was! How carefully I had protected it, or allowed it to protect me, from the pain that might otherwise have threatened it! How shaming it was that I had to visit the country where these things had been done, and go to some of the places where the murdering took place, to feel the horror of it so intensely! Did I of all people – someone who had mentally reproached his rabbinical grandfather for the gullibility with which he had held to his faith, for the near-fatal rectitude of his innocence – did I really need such 'aids' to reflection and recollection?

Apparently so.

I repeat: only one in twenty of the Jews who were living in Lithuania when the Germans invaded in 1941 was alive four years later. The Lithuanian and Latvian communities share the melancholy distinction of having had more of their people killed in the Holocaust, proportionately, than any others in Europe.

Before the war Vilnius had ninety-six synagogues; today just one remains. Strangely enough it stands on Pylimo Street, one of the city's main thoroughfares. An impressive late-nineteenth-century building, it is in the floridly Moorish style beloved (until recently) of all synagogue architects. When I went into it late one afternoon I found a group of elderly men gathering for the evening service. In figure, face, voice and gesture, in the tilt of their headgear, even in the shapes their conversational huddles had formed, they looked exactly as they should have: forlornly few in number and yet at ease too, knowing themselves to be in what was the right place, for them. I declined the invitation extended by one of their number to stay for the service. For this I was repaid, from somewhere close to the brim of his squashed hat, by a single, mock-reproachful wag of his forefinger.

In Kaunas the sole surviving synagogue is almost as large and prominently situated as the one in Vilnius. It too is more or less Moorish in style, and has a particularly fine wooden Ark of the Law at its eastern end. When my son and I went into it, early one afternoon, only the beadle was haunting the place. It was a hot day and he was jacketless. The sleeves of his white shirt were firmly buttoned at the wrists. A *yarmulke* hung on to his springy grey head of hair, as if sustained by the sheer power of prayer, with no clips to help it. He had a mild voice and a small but ready smile, and he was plainly delighted to have some company. We had quite a long conversation – he speaking in Yiddish and I responding in my fractured German, with the occasional English or Yiddish word thrown in. He told me how his parents had survived (both of them had been called into the Soviet army before the war broke out – his mother was a nurse – and had fled with their units before the advancing Germans); where he had been born (in Kaunas, two years after the war had ended); what he had done before taking over as beadle of the *shul* (driven a lorry); and how much he wished he could afford to visit his brother (who had gone to live in Israel in the 1970s). Having learned that I was from England, he also broke the news to me that the England football team had been forced to a one-all draw with Switzerland in the opening game of the European Nations' Cup, which had taken place the day before.

'They have time to do better later,' he said consolingly.

I asked him why the Germans had not destroyed the building. He responded with a characteristic shrug, a national shrug, one that contracted his shoulders and brought them up almost to his ears, while the palms of his hands spread open in front of him. All he knew was that the synagogue had been used during the war as a storeroom. Then the Russians had come and put it to the same purpose. Only in recent years had it been restored. When everything was cleared away the Ark of the Law had been found, looking just as it did now, in beautiful condition.

So the puzzle remained. In many large and small towns all over eastern Europe, the Nazis and their collaborators celebrated their conquests by herding Jews into the local synagogues, locking the doors and setting the buildings ablaze. Yet in Lithuania's two capital cities (Kaunas had served as capital of the first republic from 1921 to 1939, during the occupation of Vilnius by the Poles), they had chosen to leave these two fine structures intact. My suspicion is that they may have intended them as part of the elaborate, continent-wide 'museum' – of Jewish buildings, artefacts, pictures, books – which, in the midst of their unremitting slaughters, we know they planned to bequeath to future generations. Thus the ethnography of a vanished race would be preserved for study in centuries to come.

How could the Nazis' wish for secrecy about their crimes be reconciled with their plans for ethnographic display later? Easily! They assumed that by the time earnest *Wissenschaftler* from a variety of disciplines would come to study the materials so carefully preserved for them, the Jews would all be dead, Germany would rule the whole of Europe (if not the world), no one would have any inclination to contest her past actions and no discomfort on the subject would therefore need to be felt by anybody. Least of all by those sustaining the traditions of scrupulous and exhaustive scholarship for which the learned institutions of their country were so famous.

After all, I had seen exhibitions of an analogous nature before, though in greatly different circumstances and involving much smaller numbers of people. I refer to the San (Bushmen) of southern Africa, a hunter-gatherer people who were virtually hunted to extinction during the nineteenth century by whites, blacks and Cape Coloureds alike. Subsequently their rock paintings and carvings, their decorated ostrich eggs and stone-tipped arrows, along with drawings of them by early European travellers, were put on display in the museums of white South Africa. We used to be taken in school parties to look at these objects. No one thought to ask where the people themselves had gone; or how; or why.

*

I jumped forward in that last section, from Vilnius to Kaunas. In real life getting from the one city to the other was not so easily accomplished.

The railway timetable my son acquired at the tourist office in town turned out to have no relationship to the ones posted up at the main station; and they in turn had no apparent connection with the coming and going of trains on the platforms indicated. Signs offering *Informacia* abounded in the booking hall, but no *Informacia* was to be had from the harpies sitting in the glass boxes below. They had just one gesture for importunate foreigners: a left hand raised to ear level and flapped impatiently backwards. The large central building – complete with pink-painted Doric columns, fake marble panelling and pedimented, mahogany doorways fit for the Bank of England – was being rebuilt, so half-excavated tunnels of raw concrete and tunnels sheathed in red tiles led us nowhere. Eventually we discovered that tickets to Kaunas had to be purchased in a shed-like structure well away from the rest of the station. It was packed with a crowd of poor, depressed, expressionless, motionless, toothless people. They sat on benches ranged against the walls, their bundles on the floor beside them. A sour jumble-sale smell hung in the air, but nothing was being traded there: every out-at-elbows jacket, every bursting shoe, every bit of sticking plaster peeling away at its edges, had already found its lucky owner. Once our tickets were issued we discovered, inevitably, that we had just missed the train to Kaunas and that there would not be another for almost two hours. However, the tickets themselves were so cheap I had no inclination to complain.

Outside the station, from a sprawl of tin shacks, a noisy selling and buying of food, sweets, lottery tickets and plastic toys was going on. Stationary buses trembled in clouds of their own blue fumes. Music blared from a table piled high with tapes. Young men with nothing to do stood about in watchful groups. This scene drew from my son an approving comment:

'Well, for the first time it looks like a real capital.' However, he was not to be enticed into a brand-new McDonald's nearby; instead we went to a Stalin-era hotel on the far side of the square, where we had a Stalin-era cup of coffee. Further on was the gatehouse to the Old Town. It was a plastered, square-cut Renaissance building, adorned with black and gilt reliefs of griffins, a knight on horseback and a cross. As if to demonstrate that post-modernism was not invented yesterday, all these were topped on the same panel by a pair of jocular gates, also in relief: they would lead us to heaven presumably. On earth there was a cobbled lane running through the centre of the gatehouse, where many old women were selling, or trying to sell, rosaries and holy postcards. Other women, even older and presumably even poorer, had nothing on offer but the bowls in their hands.

My grandfather must have passed through Kaunas on his journey to and from the United States; my grandmother, I know, did the same with her family, when they were on their way to South Africa. To get to the main cross-country line from their *shtetl* they had to travel by road for about fifty miles, in a northerly direction, to Siauliai; and only then take a southbound train to Kaunas.

But Vilnius? Distant, more urbane Vilnius? Not once had I ever heard anyone in the family speak of it as a place visited by themselves or relatives. Sophisticates inside or outside Lithuania might have been free to think of the entire country as nothing more than an out-of-the-way province of the Russian empire; and of Russia itself as a kind of back yard of the continental west. But not the people from whom I was descended.

Not until I actually visited Lithuania did I become aware of just how provincial, in the most literal sense of the word, had been the life led by my forebears. Unwitting testimony to this effect, I realized while I was there, had been provided by the Introduction to my great-grandfather's BOOK, with its allusions to his pious ancestors, teachers and contemporaries. To read those few pages is to enter a world in which a place like Siauliai is a metropolis, Telz and Kelme are major centres, and Trishick, Sukian, Varniai and Grovin are assumed to be points of reference instantly recognizable by all. *That* was the family's habitat. Those were the places that mattered to it.

For them even Kaunas was out of sight. Until, in the manner of all poverty-stricken migrants, they leapt over such towns, *en route* to places incomparably further afield, like the United States or South Africa.

[14]

In Kaunas we met our guide. I shall call him Shlomo. His name and phone number had been given to me by a colleague at the university I taught at in London. A short, plump, demi-shaven bachelor approaching middle age, he was recognizable by the yellow and white baseball cap he had warned me he would be wearing. It had the legend TOTO on it (in blue Hebrew lettering) and was an advertising item given out by the Israel National Lottery. He had acquired it during his one visit to that country many years before, and hung on to it ever since. His outfit included also a short-sleeved T-shirt with green and white hoops, a pair of creased pink trousers and the inevitable trainers below. On his back was a small canvas bag, slung by a strap over a shoulder; in the rear pocket of his trousers a wallet stuffed with Lithuanian banknotes and the visiting cards of past clients.

When he talked he was all noise and bustle, interspersed with generous gestures and outbursts of scraping laughter from the back of his throat. That was his manner even when he spoke, as he often had to, of terrible scenes and events. When he was immobile, an unreachable melancholy seemed to take hold of him. Silent, he was like another person. His mouth hung a little open, the lines around it deepened, his chin seemed to sink down on itself and an abstracted, greenish glint appeared in his brown eyes. He had a characteristic way of standing then, with one arm across his belly and its cupped hand supporting the elbow of the other arm, so that his chin could come to rest reflectively on his curled fingers. Like almost all the children of survivors I met, he told me that his parents had managed to flee into Russia ahead of the advancing German army. There they had eventually met one another. Now his father was dead and he and his mother lived in a flat on the outskirts of Kaunas. Once, when we came back later than we had expected from one of our excursions, I noticed that his first thought was to phone his mother and let her know that all was well.

Alternating between the relative solitude of his bachelor state and the transient intimacies of his work, he took his duties as a guide very seriously. He was proud of all he knew about Lithuania in general and its former Jewish communities in particular; proud also of the languages he had at his command (English, Yiddish, Hebrew, Russian and Lithuanian), and of the number and variety of people he had shepherded about the country. Most of his clients were Jews from the United States, Israel and South Africa, along with the occasional visitor from Britain and Latin America; he also sometimes worked with Lithuanian educational groups. His chosen description of himself, which he repeated to me with the air of a man who had given the matter careful thought, was 'the ambassador to the Jewish people'. 'The ambassador *of* the Jewish people?' I suggested, puzzled by the phrase. But he was insistent: 'No, the ambassador *to* the Jewish people.' I did not pursue the discussion further, but I wondered on whose behalf, exactly, he saw himself carrying out his ambassadorial duties. The Jews still living in Lithuania? The dead who so vastly outnumbered them?

I suspect the latter. Even in some of the characteristics I have described as peculiar to him, Shlomo was like several other Jews I met in Lithuania. In their demeanour there was a curiously baffled attentiveness which made me think of deaf persons listening for sounds they will never hear. They moved in a strange vacancy that seemed to lie within them and yet belonged also to the world outside themselves. It was as if they were accompanied not only by the dead but also by the never-to-be-born: all those who should have been their contemporaries and companions today, the men and women whom the dead had never been given the chance of conceiving, bearing, nourishing and bringing to adulthood.

There he was, anyway, the ambassador to the Jewish people, myself included, and I was not going to dispute his title with him. The language he was proudest of, and which he fell back on whenever he was stuck for an English word or phrase, was not his parents' Yiddish, but Hebrew. So far as I could judge, his knowledge of it – of the roots of words, complex grammatical points, Israeli slang – was remarkable; and especially so as he had learned it in 'the old Soviet days', when the study of the language had been forbidden. So how had he come by it? Well, he had met an old Jew in Kaunas who had been a Hebrew teacher before the war and had studied with him. He had also once been in Odessa for a holiday and there he had met another old Jew eager to teach it to him. And finally, when things got easier, even before the Russians left, he had spent five weeks in Israel, when he had acquired his cap and much else besides. Had he not been tempted to stay there, I asked. He solemnly answered that *this* (pointing down at the Lithuanian roadway we were walking along) was his place; and *that* (pointing ahead, like a guide) was his job. Then, for the first time, I heard him describe himself as 'the ambassador to the Jewish people'.

He was to prove himself an indispensable ambassador for us. He had done his homework. Though no one before me had ever asked for his help in getting to Varniai, my grandfather's little town, or to Kelme, my great-grandfather's bigger one, he had discovered that in each of them there remained 'one last

Jew' whom we should make it our business to meet. Which in due course we did. He also took us to places we would never have found without his help, among them those overgrown double tracks through the woods that led to some of the numberless, nameless, fenced-off areas, each with a dated stone inside it, which marked what he invariably called a 'mass massacre' site.

It was clear from the way he said the two words that he firmly believed 'mass' and 'massacre' to be organically connected to one another, through a common root. Who could blame him for the error? Or would choose to correct it?

For twenty years, between the two world wars, Kaunus had been the capital of the first independent republic of Lithuania. Its departed glory showed most strikingly in the plethora of busts and full-length figures which adorned the city's open spaces. Some of the smaller parks were like open-air galleries which admitted one genre of work only: noble heads in bronze or marble. Since not a single name carved into any of the plinths or pedestals was known to us, my son took to referring to them all, collectively and satirically, as 'famous Lithuanians'. We could not even figure out what they were famous for, except in the case of the musicians, who had gilt staves or musical instruments helpfully incised on their pedestals.

Aside from a few early rulers of the country like Gediminas or Jagiello (after whom the Jagiellonian University in Poland is named), the only publicly honoured name from the past I actually recognized anywhere was that of Adam Mickiewicz, author of the Byronic/Pushkinian epic *Pan Tadeusz*. Even that act of recognition, however, had a particular irony built into it. Though he was Lithuanian-born, Mickiewicz was actually a Pole, not a Lithuanian; he wrote in the Polish language and was a member of a quasi-aristocratic class of landowning Poles who dominated the country's intellectual and political life from the seventeenth century onwards, in a style reminiscent of the Anglo-Irish Ascendancy in Ireland. This Ascendancy, however, was itself later compelled to endure centuries of subjection to the hated rule of the Tsars.

While in Vilnius I had tried unsuccessfully to get into Mickie-wicz's house, now a museum, in an ancient little courtyard in the Old Town. I had also looked out, in vain, for signs honouring another name familiar to me before I had entered the country: that of Czeslaw Milosz, the Nobel Prize-winning poet and essayist, who had gone into exile in the United States during the years of Soviet occupation. In his autobiography, *Native Realm*, Milosz plangently evokes the remote Lithuanian land-scapes of his childhood; he also describes, in loving, scornful fashion, the melancholy beauties and oddities of old Vilnius. ('Narrow cobble-stoned streets and an orgy of baroque . . .') But did Milosz, born in Lithuania, educated as a passionately bookish, Francophile Pole, ever bring himself to read any works in the language of the Lithuanians who lived around him? If so, he never mentions it.

A moment ago I drew an analogy between exhibitions I had seen in museums in South Africa and the Nazis' plans for preserving memorabilia of the Jewish life they had themselves destroyed. The 'famous Lithuanians' on display in Kaunas reminded me of South Africa yet again: of the Afrikaners in this case – another proud but despised group, cherishing a language and culture which they knew to be looked down on by their white, English-speaking compatriots (*their* Ascend-ancy).

No doubt I shall be returning to South Africa later, for further analogies and distinctions.

We had checked into the Hotel Neris immediately on arriving in Kaunas. When I told Shlomo we were staying there he expressed his approval of the arrangement in properly ambassadorial fashion. He said, 'I have good relations with the Hotel Neris.'

I can hardly make the same claim for myself. It was like another of the monuments which abounded in Kaunas: one dedicated in this case not to a 'famous Lithuanian' but to the hopeless imbecility of the Communist regime. During my several days and nights there I would find myself brooding over the question of what was to be done with the hotel now. Demolish it? Then scores of people would be put out of the subsidized non-jobs they were still hanging on to. Keep it going? Then nothing more comfortable – or profitable – or sensible – would ever replace it.

But can one imagine a 'sensible' Hilton? Or a 'sensible' Sheraton?

Step inside the Hotel Neris, at any time of day or night, and you are at once back in the Moscow of thirty years ago. It is a huge building, ten storeys high, built out of a grey concrete which is glazed over, as if with egg white, to resemble granite. Inside the foyer no guests are to be seen, only members of staff smoking cigarettes and conversing in obscure corners. A sour, singed smell rises from the threadbare carpeting. The colour scheme is mostly rotten-orange green and cyanide blue. Towels, sheets and curtains in the bedroom you are consigned to are indistinguishable from one another: all mysteriously manage to feel rough and slimy at the same time. One light bulb in six (I counted) is in working order along the endless, silent corridors. The ceiling of the 'restaurant', a room big enough for an all-Soviet Communist Party congress in the days of its omnipotence, is held up by pillars tiled from top to bottom in mirrors about a foot square each. At least half of them are cracked; many are missing. The cardboard ceiling is stained with damp and peeling away in various places. Illumination comes fitfully from brown glass globes with brass belts around their waists; from below the globes hang brass knobs like polyps awaiting surgery. Some of the globes are supported by pillars rising from the floor; others, bigger still, with wider belts and bigger knobs, are suspended from funnel-shaped apertures (also tiled with mirrors) in the ceiling. All are surrounded by stiff, seaweed-shaped, plastic flounces, at least six inches wide, three feet long and of a brown, semi-transparent colour.

Not that we had been allowed to eat amid these splendours when we first checked in. Instead we were sent to a tiny room on the ground floor in which were jammed a counter, two tables and two women who stood over us while we ate the bread and herring they produced. Then a third employee eased himself into the available space and began, not six inches from my left ear, to hammer a piece of plywood over a hole in the counter. Later I also saw placards and arrows pointing guests towards yet another 'café' on the third floor; but after traversing about a mile of unpeopled corridor all I found was a padlocked door and a sign reading 'Closed for Hygienic Reasons'.

During the time we stayed in the hotel I doubt if as many as a score of visitors came and went. Of these, no less than eight belonged to a single American family, the father Lithuanian-born, the mother and children not, who had come over to visit his parents. The impression made by his dependants was one of well-disciplined unhappiness. With just two exceptions, the other guests were tough-looking local males, always in pairs or trios. One of them, a big, sallow-faced creature dressed all in black – suit, tie, hat, sunglasses – approached us a few times to make *sotto voce* propositions, but as he spoke only Russian and Lithuanian we had no idea what he was offering us. The only spot of colour in his ensemble was a red oval sticker on the left-hand lens of his glasses. It said RAY-BAN. Evidently he wanted the world to know that he was not one to put up with cheap local rubbish. The two other guests were a Canadian woman diplomat, six feet high, and a male colleague, who stayed one night only. At breakfast I heard her saying apologetically to him, 'I used to go in for all that heavy-drinking stuff in my twenties. That was in the old Soviet days. We didn't have any work to do then.'

For these desultory souls, and ourselves, the entire ten-storey establishment was kept going. At all times staff greatly outnumbered guests. Cleaners gossiped over their motionless brooms; receptionists played cards and drank tea in a room behind the foyer; sounds of vehement, multi-sided arguments issued from invisible persons in the kitchen. My son and I even had our own personal *dezhurnaya*, an elderly woman of the usual dejected appearance and copious dimensions, who sat at her desk near the lift and looked after the floor we had entirely to ourselves. There was also a youth employed to guard the back gate, who spent his nights in a little hut out there. I think he was mad; perhaps he thought the same of me. He had a tape-player attached to a powerful electronic amplifier, from which Lithuanian pop would emerge at rock-concert volume any hour he fancied – midnight, 2 a.m., 4 a.m, 6 a.m. Then I would lean out of the window of the room, wait for a moment's silence and yell into the darkness, 'Shut up! *Ruhe! Tais-toi!*' and anything else that occurred to me. Sometimes my yells were effective; more often not. Once, from four floors below, a policeman responded to my cries by saying to me in English, in conversational tones, 'I will see to it, sir. There is no problem.' But the racket broke out again an hour later. The most effective intervention was achieved by my son, who finally had the wit to go to the *dezhurnaya* and ask her to do something about it. She proved to be much more effective at frightening him off than the policeman.

It was many years since Simon and I had spent so much time alone in one another's company. Despite the low threshold of irritability which each of us accused the other of having, we got on without squabbles or sulks. Born and raised in England, casual in manner, self-reliant by temperament, my older son has spent many years living in non-English-speaking countries, and he delighted the Lithuanians by making generous use of the phrases in their language which he rapidly mugged up from a guidebook. This, coming from an English-speaking visitor, or perhaps from any visitor, was clearly a novelty to them. He also constantly went off on his own, by day and night; on one of these outings he met a couple from France who were on some kind of exchange visit, and their Lithuanian hostess, a woman a few years younger than himself; subsequently he spent time with them not only in Vilnius but in Kaunas too.

All this helped to keep us on good terms with one another. So did the history we were exploring. Looking back, I am not surprised by the fact that we talked so little about it while we were there. We did not need to. I remember an occasion when we 'lost' one another in the centre of Vilnius – I walked one way, he another, and when I looked around for him he was gone. Back and forth I went, expecting to see him around every corner: not knowing where he had got to, why it had happened, how we could be failing to find one another. It was incomprehensible. I was not so much alarmed by his disappearance as bewildered. It was morning; the streets were not crowded; no ambulance or police sirens sounded. Eventually I decided to carry on with what I had planned to do: to visit the university and then go to a bank before returning to the hotel. We were both adults; he could look after himself as well as I could. As time passed, however, the indecision and bewilderment I had felt earlier turned into depression; depression into a sense of desolation. This was nothing. He would come back. We would find each other again. But all those others – !

We met up again at the hotel a few hours later. Having gone through a similar experience on his side, Simon said, 'It was weird. I couldn't understand where you'd got to.' Looking up, he opened his mouth in a strange grimace that had something of a shudder in it: '*Here!*'

Smaller than its equivalent in Vilnius, Kaunas Old Town is also less disrupted by new roads and parking lots. Its main pedestrian promenade is a jostle of architectural styles from the fifteenth century onwards; its side streets are short and shabby. All are steeped in subdued tints that pulse slowly in the midsummer Baltic light, during the evenings especially. The Town Hall Square is positively grand, and not the less so for having a low terrace of late-medieval buildings huddled along one side of it. If the square and the churches nearby were all picked up and moved 500 miles to the west they would be surrounded by cordons of tour buses; the cobbled piazza would be littered with reclining backpackers; the medieval buildings would be transformed into shops selling lavender bags, glassware, oatmeal soaps and handknitted sweaters. Instead the whole area is empty every evening. Only one small bar is open. Children play ball games in the vacant spaces. Bells ring. Now a couple of housewives cross the square, their slippers scuffling on the stones. Then it is the turn of an old priest and a young one. Their shoes go clop-clop, in ecclesiastical measure.

We leave them behind us and walk towards the confluence of the Neris and Nemunas rivers. The houses on the far side of the square, and beyond it, are more handsome and even more dilapidated than those we have already seen. When they come to an end we find ourselves on a sandy path running through grass and shrubs, just a foot or two above the water-line. Both rivers are empty of boats. Light holds steady on the sliding water, though the sun has long since gone.

At the confluence the path curves back towards a dismantled church and a medieval brick fortress. The fort's outer buildings and walls could be those of a neglected farm; its keep is circular and topped by a pointed, hat-like iron roof. Two women are walking ahead of us; one is young, one middle-aged; they are talking in English, though it is the mother tongue of neither; both are smartly dressed, in soft blouses and pale, long skirts which are clearly not of Lithuanian origin. I hear the younger woman say, 'Joseph Brodsky is also dead, is he not?' A group of young people now comes towards us, half a dozen of them, men and women. They are laughing and talking loudly, but are apparently not so preoccupied with one another as to overlook our foreignness, or Jewishness, or both. They have gone several yards past when I hear, not for the first time since my arrival in Lithuania, elaborate hawking and throat-clearing followed by a violent expectoration. What I then hear is wholly unfamiliar. It is the sound of the gob falling just behind my back foot. Given the distance between us, and given the fact that the spitter would have had to turn 180 degrees in order to direct his mouthful in our direction, this cannot be accidental. Simon says, 'He's just doing it to show off.' I argue that he did it because I am a Jew. It may also be that to have passed two groups of foreigners speaking English, one after the other, had been too much for his sensitive soul to bear.

Back to the square. Back to the gracious town hall. It is known (or so the guidebook claims) as the White Swan, because of its white walls and elegantly tall white tower. Another kind of 'guidebook' to Kaunas (*The Kovno Ghetto Diary of Avraham Tory*) tells me some less gracious things about the uses to which this building has been put. Like so many others in Kaunas. On occasion.

Fort IX stands two or three miles outside Kaunas. On one side of it is a new-looking suburb; on the other, the cross-country motorway to the coast. More than 30,000 people were murdered in or near the fort between 1941 and 1944. Their remains lie in a field barely 100 yards to the south of the buildings. When you turn your back on it you see the skyline of Kaunas at a distance; though not a great one. If you gaze across the field you see half-made constructions approaching from the west – from the direction any invading German army would have to take.

For its size, which is modest enough, Fort IX has enclosed within itself as much evildoing as any place on earth. I cannot think of any other words to describe the building and its surroundings, though I know that evil can never be quantified or aggregated. It can only be inflicted and suffered: inflicted by individuals, whether they do it from a distance or in the presence of their victims; suffered by individuals whose bodies and minds are always the true site, the only site, of what is done to them. In Lithuania and the countries adjacent to it there are literally thousands of places like Fort IX about which the same story can be told, from the same period and to the same effect. Some of their names are infamous; they have become metonyms for an entire epoch. Most are completely unknown.

And further afield? Over a longer time-span? Only the globe's most uninhabitable wastes remain wholly innocent and undefiled.

In the late nineteenth century the Russians built a series of twelve forts around Kaunas to enable them to defend the city against the German armies which they knew would sooner or later invade the country. In 1914 the Germans duly appeared and the forts promptly surrendered, for all their size and complexity, the thickness of their walls, the size and number of their cannon, the depth of their tunnels and underground chambers, the cunning lines of their earthworks and the elevated positions on which they had been built. Subsequently several of them fell into disuse. Others did not. Between the wars the government of the first Lithuanian republic turned Forts IV, VII and IX into prisons for its enemies: some criminals; many Communists. When the Russians returned in 1939 they also, predictably enough, used them as prisons: for anti-Communists, members of the local intelligentsia, Zionists etc. Then, from mid-1941 to early 1945, it was the Germans' turn once again. They used the forts as headquarters, torture chambers and places of mass slaughter. Of the three, Fort IX had the most horrific reputation – which is to say only that more innocent people, the overwhelming majority of them Jews, were killed there than at the other sites in and near the city.

When the Russians came back in 1944 they did not (so far as I know) again put Fort IX to use as a prison. Instead they built two memorials near it. The bigger of the two looks at first sight like just another piece of Stalinist bombast: it reminded me of the crushingly oversize war memorials that stand outside Kiev and other Russian cities. Closer up, however, the distorted torsos, faces and clenched fists of the figures, which rise out of what might be splintered tree trunks, or perhaps the muzzles of shattered cannon, do convey a genuine sense of torment, outrage and despair, as well as the defiant and triumphalist sentiments indispensable to all public monuments erected during the Soviet era. Dedicated to 'victims of fascism', the memorial says not a word about the Jews.

The other, smaller memorial nearby is dedicated specifically to the soldiers of the Red Army who lost their lives in retaking Kaunas. It consists of dart-shaped flanges of concrete rising not much higher than the slope they rest on. The points of the darts are aimed straight at the fort, as if striking at it from the east – from the direction any invading Russian army would have to take.

On the day we were there, this monument had been transformed by some adolescent boys into a skateboarding arena.

A woman took our tickets at the entrance to the fort. We passed through a small grassy yard, with barbed wire running around the top of high brick walls on three sides of it. The fourth side of the rectangle consisted of a flank of the fort itself.

It was a hot June day; but a single step inside the fort and the sweat on my skin felt like ice. It was colder still downstairs, in the basement, where the corridor and cells were awash with two or three inches of dirty water. Boarded walkways had been put down on the floors, but the opening and closing of every door sent a small tide sloshing back and forth. This was in midsummer; and a dry one too. What is it like, what was it like, during the Lithuanian winter? The only light came from some dim bulbs and a few barred, semicircular apertures let into the outer walls of the cells. These were large chambers, set along one side of the corridor, each perhaps twenty-five feet long and half that in width. Dark, foully cold and sopping wet though they were, oppressed on all sides by brutish weights of brick, concrete and heavy steel, the basement contained even worse places than these. Two holes cut into the walls had served as 'punishment cells'. Punishment cells! There! One was a black, windowless, tubular tunnel no more than three or four feet high and less than that in width. It had no lighting of any kind. The other, also windowless, also without light, also fitted with a black, blank door, had for its ceiling a steel staircase leading to the level above. So those thrown into its pitch darkness were tormented at all hours by the thunder of boots and wooden clogs on reverberating steel just a few inches above their heads.

To this place, to these cells, the Nazis dragged not only thousands of Jews from Kaunas and its neighbourhood, but thousands more from much greater distances – people of any age and both sexes brought across the width of Europe and kept here for days, freezing, starving, crushed together as they had been in the cattle trucks they had travelled in, before being taken 100 yards outside the fort and shot. They began these transports from Germany and Austria in November 1941; as late as May 1944, when the war was clearly lost, when the advancing Soviet armies were not far from recapturing Vilnius, when Himmler, the commander of the SS, had himself begun to wonder – at that stage! – if he might manage to save his own skin by calling off the Final Solution (as though, Hannah Arendt wrote, 'it had been a joke') – *even then* his underlings and their collaborators of all kinds found the will and means to drag a trainload of 900 French Jews from Paris to Kaunas, to incarcerate them in Fort IX and then to do to them what they had already done to so many others.

In the cell at one end of the underground corridor the wall-scratchings of these French prisoners, now preserved behind glass, can still be seen. 'Nous sommes neuf cents Français,' one of them had cut into the plaster, anonymously enough. Also, among many others, were 'Lob, Marcel, Mai 1944'; 'Wechsler, Abram, de Limoges – Paris, 18.5.44'; 'Max Stern, Paris, 18.5.44'; 'Herskovits L'Anvers de Monaco via Drancy Paris, Kaunas'. Perhaps most affecting of all – if such a distinction is not itself a shaming one to make, in such a context – is the inscription 'A.J. Feinberg de Paris 12'. As who should say: John Smith of London NW1.

The cells in the floor above have now been largely turned into another museum of suffering: most, but not all of it, Jewish. There is part of a cell devoted (neutrally, as it were) to the history of the fort from its inception; another serves as a memorial to the Lithuanians who were imprisoned or killed there by the Russians, during their brief period of rule between the formal extinction of the first Lithuanian republic in 1940 and the arrival of the Germans a year later. Then there are sections dealing with the wholesale murder of the Jews of Kaunas within the first few months of the capture of the city; the subsequent imprisonment of the survivors ('work Jews') in the ghetto; the destruction of the countryside communities; the resistance to their fate offered by Jewish partisans; the shelter provided to handfuls of fugitives by Righteous Gentiles. Part of yet another cell is devoted to the planning and execution of a break-out from the fortress by sixty Jewish workers who, after it had become apparent to the German high command that victory was no longer a certainty, were assigned the task of digging up and burning the corpses of the dead. (Of this, more below.) Finally, photographs and photocopied documents celebrate the actions of a man by the name of Senpo Sugihara, the Japanese Consul in Kaunas between the Germans' invasion of Poland in 1939 and their subsequent assault on the Soviet Union in 1941. On his own authority, and at considerable risk to himself, Sugihara issued no less than 6,000 visas to Jews who had just fled from Poland and found temporary refuge in Kaunas. These visas permitted the lucky holders to enter Japan – which meant that they were permitted to cross the Soviet Union *en route*, and thus make good their escape.

Once again then, wall after wall of pictures of doomed Jews: some at school in the Kaunas Ghetto, some sitting in councils, some in the woods with rifles in their hands, uncountable others already dead. Then a glass case of items dug up from the 'mass massacre' site nearby. Bunches of keys lie among them (householders had naturally locked the doors of their homes before they left, as anyone would); penknives; spectacles and spectacles cases; combs; purses; a pair of lady's scissors; a tiny, dusty, intact pair of shoes – the shoes of a two-year-old, I would guess, his or her first 'real' shoes, with buttonholes in the straps across the ankles, and little buttons to be pushed through them.

It was a relief, a shaky relief, but a relief nevertheless, to get out of the building and go wandering over the western outskirts of the fort. The sunny slopes and shaded hollows on that side of it were all man-made, the product of Tsarist tunnelling and trenching. Placid grass and a multitude of wild flowers covered them completely. Out of the green hummocks and dips there emerged at random, like so many ungainly fossils, an occasional dome or doorway roofed in concrete three feet thick.

On the other side of the fort was the paved walkway to the largest of the massacre sites and, beyond that, the Soviet monument to the dead described above. Lying flat on the ground next to the walkway were inscribed tablets from different phases of post-1945 Lithuanian history. The original one put down by the Communists does not mention Jews at all; another does so as if they were just a small percentage of the dead; another, the most recent, in Lithuanian, Yiddish, Russian and English, finally comes clean, so to speak, and makes it plain that by far the greatest number of the people slaughtered here were Jews: THIS IS THE PLACE WHERE NAZIS AND THEIR ASSISTANTS KILLED MORE THAN 30,000 JEWS FROM LITHUANIA AND OTHER EUROPEAN COUNTRIES.

I was to discover later that the reference to the Nazis' 'helpers' or 'assistants' was a standard formula, used on monuments to the Jewish dead all over the country; I learned also that the wording had been arrived at only after strenuous arguments between the government of the post-Soviet Lithuanian republic and its small Jewish community. The government had wanted these inscriptions to refer to the killers simply as 'Nazis'; the Jews had insisted that the inscriptions should speak of 'the Nazis and their Lithuanian assistants'. But that plea was not accepted. So even the latest and last inscriptions had not come entirely clean, after all.

'We said to the government,' I was told by someone at a comparable, 'small-scale' site elsewhere, 'we said to them – this is the falsification of history all over again – you are behaving exactly like the Stalinists. But they would not listen to us. So these words were agreed. It had to be just "assistants". Nothing "Lithuanian" about them.'

He dropped the hand he had stretched out to me, its fingers gathered together at their tips, the better for passionate gesturing. His voice tailed off, like a man acknowledging defeat. 'A *kompromis*.'

Standing at the memorial tablets, you overlook directly the field of the dead. It is two or three acres in extent, with a tilt down to the south and west. Plentifully sprinkled with the season's flowers – daisies, knapweed, forget-me-nots, bird's-foot trefoil, dandelions – most of it is covered by the tall, heavy-headed grass of mid-June which the breeze keeps in constant motion: bowing, rising, stirring, settling momentarily. So thick is the grass that whenever a stronger gust blows you would think the sun has gone behind a small cloud and a shadow is crossing the field from right to left. But it is only the light striking the heavy heads of seed at a different angle from before.

The sky is clear, all the way to the horizon. The new blocks of flats in the suburb to the west approach inexorably.

In the fort – a visitor merely, a sightseer – I had felt simply:

let me out of here; this is intolerable; I can't breathe. It was much easier outside, under the sky, in the fresh air, looking over the grass. Yet it was here, on this shining slope, with all the specks and sparks of dusk already flying about in the near-horizontal rays of the declining sun, that events which can be neither imagined nor forgotten had taken place: day after day, month after month, for three years on end.

And even then the killers were not content. They could not leave their victims in the peace of the indiscriminate grave into which they had flung them. Towards the end of 1943 they ordered the entire field to be dug up and the corpses buried in it to be exhumed and burned. Naturally they employed squads of Jews for the task, all of whom were to be shot once the job was finished. The process had begun much earlier elsewhere in eastern Europe, once the German high command had realized that it was possible, after all, that they were not going to emerge as victors from this war. An order was therefore given to a special detachment of the SS to supervise the destruction of the evidence of the crimes they had committed during the occupation.

So how did they go about it at Fort IX? By ordering the cremation (on petrol-drenched railway sleepers) of thousands of corpses on the outskirts of Lithuania's second-largest city! Screens of white cloth were erected to conceal what was going on from houses no more than half a mile away. The idea that nobody would divine the meaning of this activity, of the flames, smoke and smell, at that place of all places, as the Russian armies drew nearer – and that no one would survive to talk of it afterwards – is yet another aspect of the craziness of the crimes committed there. It is also a further example of the infernal tenacity which, to the very end, was to mark every stage of the Final Solution. Later still, as the German forces made their final retreat along the eastern front, from the Baltic countries in the north to Hungary and Yugoslavia in the south, they drove ahead of them hundreds of thousands of starving slave labourers of all nationalities, among them Russians and Poles in large numbers, as well as those Jews who had somehow managed to escape the gas chambers. They sent them out in midwinter on 'death marches' or crammed them into open railway trucks and dispatched them on journeys to nowhere across shattered railway networks.

This was not to hide the evidence of their criminality: it was to blazon it abroad. *They could not let go.* By then all that remained of the power exercised for so long by the Nazi state and the Nazi war machine in all its parts – SS, Security Police, Order Police, regular army units, Baltic and Ukrainian militias – was the helplessness of these dying people; the only 'vindication' innumerable commanders and other ranks could now offer themselves of the crimes they had committed was the commission of more crimes yet. From the speeches and statements of those directly responsible for organizing, supervising and executing the Final Solution, from Himmler downwards, there is no doubt that they knew the slaughtering of millions of unarmed people of all ages, and from every quarter of the continent, to have been a deed of an unparalleled foulness. From those documents it is also clear that this consciousness of guilt, if it can be so called, actually excited them to further deeds of the same sort. Their crime was so enormous, so pointless, it cost them so little and accomplished so much, it had convinced them that only a species of giant could have been entrusted with it and have succeeded in carrying it out. In their own consciousness each of them, like that miserable Jaeger of *Einsatzkommando* 3, had made of himself nothing less than a *welthistorische* figure.

If you wanted to see his monument look around you.

All this was as true of this later phase of what was done here, outside Kaunas, as it was of any other. The victims of Fort IX were dead, but still the killers could not let them go. They had to have their bodies dug up so that they could be desecrated all over again. They had to use for the task Jewish slaves who were themselves doomed to death and incineration once the task was done.

One squad assigned to digging up and cremating the dead at Fort IX managed to plan and execute an extraordinarily elaborate break-out. It involved fabricated keys, bars, chains and steel doors sawn through with stolen files, the excavation of forgotten tunnels and the digging of new ones. Shlomo took us along the route they had followed. Earlier, in one of the cells, we had seen a display of charts and pictures relating to this escape; and a proud, melancholy photo of a post-war reunion of the survivors. Only about ten of the more than sixty men who had made the break-out appear in it. There were no escapees from any of the squads that had preceded them or from the squads that took their place.

[16]

I have never seen more deceitfully innocent-looking landscapes than those of Lithuania. True, I was there late in June, at the peak of the summer, when every growing thing was as thick, tall, green and succulent as it ever would be. But it was not that alone which gave the countryside its almost trance-like appearance of trust and openness. It was, rather, the feature of it that had surprised me from the moment I arrived in the country: the absence of visible demarcations within it. Outside the towns and villages there were virtually no wire fences, no hedges, no palings, no stone walls, no recognizable signs indicating where one man's property ended and another's began. Here, it seemed, they were confident their neighbours would not trespass on their lands, their cattle not trample down the fields of wheat and rye which lay about unprotected everywhere, their flocks of goats or sheep not devour the vegetable beds available to them.

How could this be? It turned out that there was a simple answer to this question, at least where the animals were concerned. There was no need to fear damage from herds of cattle or flocks of sheep because the Lithuanians did not appear to have any. One cow at a time was the rule here; two or three goats; no sheep at all. These animals were always kept tied to a post or to the trunk of a tree, generally within yards of the nearest farmstead. Munching in the sun or lying in the shade, they looked wholly at peace with their lot, like creatures taken straight out of eighteenth-century etchings of rural life. Once a cow had eaten a circle around itself, it would be led by a boy or a girl to a different tree, with a virginal area of grass around it, and tied up there for a new meal to begin. Calves were not tied up at all; it was left to them to stick close to their mothers, which they always did, and to follow them obediently home when, towards evening, they were dragged away for milking.

No flocks, no herds: no need for fences therefore. Hence the open, innocent appearance of the countryside, as if entire historical periods had been bypassed and an earlier period preserved: one that predated not only the Communist collectivizations but pre-industrial enclosures as well. Some lands, I was told, remain in collective ownership still, though the process of returning them to individual farmers has begun; if so, the difference between private and collective land is impossible for a stranger to discern. Even the railway lines were seldom fenced off. If you happened to live in one of the arthritic wooden cottages along the line, and wanted to catch the train, you simply stood next to the line and flagged it down. If it was the non-express kind of train on which my son and I found ourselves, it stopped. The cow or goat in the nearest orchard looked on placidly: it presented no danger to the train, and vice versa.

In front of these rail-side cottages were circular, concrete-lined wells with little tents of wood or concrete over them. Then a scrappy, unpicturesque village would appear, built for the most part of a near-universal, sandy-looking brick. Then more flat, fenceless fields of wheat, rye or barley; more orchards (apples mostly); berries on canes; beans on stakes; cauliflowers and cabbages growing fat on the ground; another wooden cottage with fretwork ornamentation along its eaves; grassy plains dotted with wild flowers. No mountains; barely anything resembling a hill; slow-flowing rivers; stretches of woodland; a substantial tree-fringed lake or two – and that was it, as far as 'features' went. Tilting this way and that, falling into small depressions and rising sedately out of them, the plains looked silvery in hue, compared with the darker, stronger greens of cultivated crops; the woods were darker still; newly ploughed or sown fields almost black; the horizon a tenuous blue, just distinguishable from the blue of the sky. Thick clumps of lupins grew like weeds all over the place, their individual flowers so big and so purple I wondered if they were not a cultivated variety that had somehow escaped from captivity and gone feral, like rabbits in Australia or cats on South Georgia Island.

Nor were the stretches of woodland or forest nearly as dark and sinister as I had thought they would be; at least not in the regions I travelled through. They were less extensive too. I had pictured mile after mile of sombre, unbroken pine and birch, and little else. But none of the woods I saw ever took over the landscape entirely. Oak and sycamore abounded, along with lime and ash, alder and poplar. They looked altogether friendlier, gentler, more midsummer-night's-dreamy than my childhood imaginings had led me to expect. Like so much else seen from the windows of the cars, trains or buses we travelled on, they seemed to cloak themselves in an insidious literary-moralistic mist, a pictorial-aesthetic haze.

The same was true of the tasks people could be seen carrying out in these rural areas. A woman draws water from a well outside her cottage. Men and women scythe grass together and heap it up in beehive-shaped stacks. A man harrows a field behind a single horse. A family group kneels together to weed a large patch of vegetables. A solitary girl carries harvested fruit (berries?) home in a large basket. A man flicks his whip at a mule, his coffin-shaped wagon trundling along behind him. Dwarfed by the ploughed field ahead of her, a woman scatters seed out of a bag slung over her shoulder.

*

One of the stops we made was at a 'museum' established in the middle of nowhere by a late-eighteenth-century 'Lithuanian cultural worker and writer' by the name of Dionyz Poshka. To get to it we travelled along an unmade road that ran through a landscape a little hillier than usual; skirted a small hidden lake in front of a manorial-looking house and a plantation of lime trees; crossed a sort of causeway; and finally emerged from the car with a slam of doors that sent conclaves of skullcapped, prelatical crows cawing and flapping in all directions. For some reason (viral? seasonal? genetic?) the ground was thickly littered with their fallen feathers, as if in a parody of autumn. The most recently fallen of the feathers were black; the oldest white; between them could be found every shade of businessmen's suiting.

The museum consists, in its entirety, of the stump of a huge, upright, hollow oak tree and a modern wood and glass shelter built around it. In the open space in front a blond child is struggling to get his tricycle upright; at the sight of us he runs off to tell his mother of our arrival. She is a large, smiling woman, visitors' book in hand, to whom we pay a fee for admission. A notice (in four languages) on the shelter tells visitors about the life and works of Dionyz Poshka. It also says, 'Inside the trunk of this tree, an giant [sic] of a thousand years old, the winds used to bellow and the people called it "Baublis".'

So we take it in turns to squeeze ourselves into the museum – i.e. the hollow stump of 'Baublis'. About 200 years ago Dionyz Poshka somehow managed to insert into this space a wooden seat, a wooden table and a wooden bunk, all of his own manufacture. Amid these cramped conveniences he would write his poetry and do his cultural works, sitting or lying as the mood took him. (He owned a farmhouse for use on other occasions; it is 'at a distance of a verst', the notice tells us.) He was also a collector of 'ethnographic materials', which he kept in the tree trunk. Of these there remain a painted wooden carving of Jesus (about eighteen inches high); another wooden carving, also painted, of a devout male person (perhaps an Apostle) at prayer; and, hanging together from a hook on the wall (i.e. the trunk), a ragged bit of chain mail, like a piece torn from an old string vest, and a round metal shield the size of a soup plate. The latter items presumably represented for him the life of action, as against the *vita contemplativa* he had chosen for himself.

In the visitors' book I find that someone from County Kerry, Ireland, has written a generous tribute to his museum: 'This is the craziest place I've ever seen.' There is also a more respectful reference to the site in Mickiewicz's *Pan Tadeusz*, which was first published in 1834:

> Trees of my fatherland! If heaven will
> Shall I return and find you still?
> My friends of old, are you alive today?
> Among whom as a child I used to play;
> And is the great Baublis living found
> By ages hollowed out, in whose great round
> A dozen folk could sup as in a room?

Very thin folk, I assume.

Need I say it? Go back a few miles from the museum, leave the metalled road, enter the woods and for several hundred yards bump along a double track so narrow that the sides of the car are brushed all the way by hazel twigs and (more softly, almost as if with feather dusters) by bracken. Then get out and walk along a bramble-entangled footpath. Come to a sun-dappled, fenced-off space. A flat stone, perhaps four feet high, stands on edge within it. Incised into its top left-hand corner is a gilt Star of David. Below the star is an inscription in Yiddish and Lithuanian, with a date recording the day on which the Jews of Babtai and Vandziogela were brought here to be shot. Stand

and look around, while birds chirp and argue and agitate the leaves that conceal them from you. Walk back to the car, return to the metalled road, go forward another few miles, leave the road, travel a much shorter distance through the woods; same woods, sunlight, brambles, birdsong; same fence too, you might think; and same cleared space inside it, and up-reared stone, with the Star of David and inscription in Lithuanian and Yiddish. Only, this one bears a slightly different date and this is where the Jews of Ariogala were brought to be shot.

Return to the metalled road, go on a few more miles, enter the woods . . .

All right – stop – enough – we don't need to go and see where the Jews of Nemaksciai were shot. (I think that was the name. My notes here are hard to read.) We could spend a week, a month, like this. I want to get to my mother's Varniai.

But Shlomo was insistent that we should go and see where these particular Jews were murdered. He had his own autobiographical reasons for wanting us to see it. It was not that his family had come from there. They had been Kaunas people. He wanted us to visit the place because during his schooldays he had once camped in the woods nearby, with a group of boys from his high school. They had specialized in nature, hiking, geography, that kind of thing. 'Like a hobby group,' he explained. They had gone there during a vacation and were living under canvas. Talking with some of the local boys one evening, they learned that just a few hundred yards from their campsite was a place where Jews had been shot during the war. So the next morning Shlomo and his schoolmates were taken by the locals to see it. Even in those days, he said, the ground was cleared and there was a kind of fence around it. But no notice; no Star of David; nothing. That was the first 'mass massacre' site outside Kaunas he had seen. The location of most of the other places he learned about when he had already begun to be a guide for visitors. But not this one.

Who had put the fence around the site at that time? He did not know. Survivors perhaps. More likely the Russians had done it. They were always ready to mark the sites of Nazi atrocities, as long as the people buried there were just called 'victims of fascism'. What they could not tolerate at such places was any display of 'Jewish separatism' or 'reactionary religious sentiment' or 'Zionism'. They had plenty of such phrases at their disposal. All meant one thing only: they were intended to prohibit any mention of what the Jews, especially, had suffered.

And the boys in the camp with him? How did they respond when they came here? What did they say to him? And the local boys who had taken them to the place?

When it finally came, Shlomo's reply echoed in almost uncanny fashion the one given to me by the young woman I had met in the artists' colony in Vilnius. 'Everybody knows such things. Every place you go to, they always knew.'

So we too went, after all, to see where yet another community had been wiped out. Like the others, it was a sun-fretted clearing in the midst of a silence broken only by the conversation of birds and their scufflings about overhead and in the undergrowth. While we were there I wanted to ask Shlomo how *he* had dealt with his schoolmates after this unplanned piece of exploration; this unexpected part of their 'field trip'. But looking into the plump, sorrowing, half-comical face of the schoolboy who was now the self-appointed and self-educated ambassador to the Jewish people, I thought, the hell with it.

Before leaving I had consulted a man in the Lithuanian consulate in London about several matters, one of them being the hiring of a car and driver when I was there. At that point he suddenly became agitated. 'Gangsters! Mafiosi! Everyone a crook! You can't be too careful!' No further advice on the subject was to be got out of him.

The driver Shlomo found for us was far from being a gangster, a crook, a mafioso. Softly spoken and self-effacing, he was tall and handsome in what I now thought of as a typically Lithuanian fashion: neat, light brown hair; slender hands and cheekbones; pale, oblique eyes; a long nose; a clear, non-committal brow. By trade he was a self-employed locksmith. That was why he was able to do freelance driving whenever a job came up. He was just over forty, I would guess; about Shlomo's age, but in better physical condition. His name was Albertis. Like everything else about him, his driving was deft and self-assured. Walking, driving or eating, his manner was attentive yet detached; his movements were relaxed; he kept his voice low and his gestures discreet. He was our driver; but the car he drove, a comfortable Opel, was his own; so he had his ways of indicating degrees of independence as well as deference. Shlomo was the beneficiary of certain glances from him, movements of the hand, faint smiles; my son and I of others.

Whenever I offered him a biscuit from the packet I had prudently bought in Marks and Spencer before leaving London, he always, carefully, respectfully, took two; when we ate meals together he finished off every scrap on his plate, and would eat without embarrassment what we offered him from ours; when he wanted a smoke he left the room or retired to a distance in the open air. We also ate together ice creams in various ramshackle bus shelters, and a sweet, crumbling, maize-yellow, stalagmite-resembling substance, like a custard risen into stiff points, which Shlomo insisted was called 'pancake'. (When I objected to this name he pointed out that it was cooked in a pan and was a kind of cake: so what else could he call it?) Another item we shared was water from a flower-bedecked holy well which marked the border between the province of Samogitia and the rest of Lithuania. It turned out that Varniai itself, my destination, the town for the sake of which I had embarked on this journey, actually lay in Samogitia (though I never once heard the name from my mother or anyone else in the family). Albertis too had been born in the province; and at Shlomo's urging he treated us to the sound of the Samogitian dialect. To our ears it sounded indistinguishable from everything else Lithuanian, but Shlomo and Albertis derived much amusement from the performance.

What Catholic, Samogitian, Lithuanian Albertis thought of us, and of the other Jewish quasi-revenants from the four quarters of the globe whom he drove about the country, by arrangement with Shlomo, I will never know. I did, however, feel that I got to understand him better – or at least to see in a different light his carefully self-restrained movements and detached manner – after he had told us about the period he had spent 'in the old days' as a conscript in the submarine corps of the Soviet navy. (The conversation was conducted via Shlomo, but at a rapid rate and with much more animation than any other I had with Albertis.) He had been an 'engineer and torpedist'. Also the only Lithuanian in the crew. As a result he had often felt very lonely. 'Lonely? In a submarine?' I asked disbelievingly. 'Easy,' he answered; and from his expression and the shake of his head I took him to mean that it was 'easy' only in the sense that it was hard to avoid and harder still to endure. I asked him why they had put him into the submarine service when he was so tall. He had a one-word answer to that question too: 'Russians!' Had they given him any psychological tests beforehand? This produced the only laugh I heard from him. It was brief enough. 'Russians? If they gave you a physical you were lucky. Never mind psychology tests.' So did he suffer from claustrophobia? 'Yes, sometimes.' What did he do about it? 'Nothing.'

Most of his time at sea had been spent in the Mediterranean, shadowing the American Sixth Fleet. 'Of course they were also watching us. That's how it was.' To show us how it was, he made a St Andrew's cross directly in front of his eyes, squint-fashion. The highest state of alert they were ever put on was during the Arab-Israeli war of 1973. Had he been frightened then? He shrugged. 'Not too much frightened. Excited. We came very close to the American ships sometimes.' Now he held his index fingers upright and parallel in front of him, an inch or two apart, to show how close they had come. The best part of his service had been as a member of a team which delivered Russian submarines to the Arabs: once to the Egyptians and once to the Syrians. Then they remained ashore for months in Alexandria and Latakia, training the new crews. Afterwards they were flown back to Odessa.

With a mixture of bravado and self-pity, both softly spoken, he summed up the whole experience: 'I was young then – nearly a boy. It's a long time ago.' As if what he was about to say was harder to credit than the passing of his own youth, he added, 'Even the Russkies are gone.'

Since one occasionally reads or hears reports of Jewish memorials being overturned and daubed with swastikas in various European and Latin American countries, and since I have mentioned being spat at in Kaunas, I should say that while in Lithuania, a country befouled by the actions of many hundreds, thousands more likely, of its own people during the war, I saw no sign of any Jewish memorial being despoiled in any way. Or even a sign anywhere of its being thought necessary to protect such memorials against possible despoilment. Before new premises were found for it, the London Jewish Museum in Bloomsbury was transformed into something like a fortress; the frail little wooden box of the Jewish State Museum in Vilnius, by contrast, stands unprotected. Synagogues in London generally have their windows barred against stones, petrol bombs or worse; but not the two surviving synagogues I saw in Vilnius and Kaunas. Nothing could be more vulnerable to desecration than the Jewish 'mass massacre' sites in remote woodlands all over Lithuania; yet no harm appears to come to them. On a busy street corner in Kaunas, standing about breast high and with no railings around it, is an elegant, understated grey-blue marble monument, in shape resembling a tombstone, which marks the entrance to what was once the Nazi-created Kaunas Ghetto. No spray-painted oaths or swastikas mar it.

Some of the credit for this must go to the explicitly stated attitudes and policies of the new republican government. For various reasons, guilt not least among them, it has made formal acknowledgement of the crimes of the past and given moral support to what remains of its tiny Jewish community. (Even if, as we have seen, it has insisted on carefully euphemizing the inscriptions on the memorials it has itself put up.) Two months after the Supreme Council's declaration of the republic's independence from the Soviet Union in 1990, its first President, Vytautis Landsbergis, signed a declaration which reads in part as follows:

The Council, in the name of the Lithuanian nation, condemns the genocide committed against the Jewish people during the Nazi occupation in Lithuania, and notes with sorrow that Lithuanian citizens were among the executioners who served the occupiers. For the crime committed against the Jewish people in Lithuania and outside its borders there is not and cannot be any justification or any statute of limitations on criminal prosecutions. The Republic of Lithuania will not tolerate any display of antisemitism.

The reference to the Lithuanian 'executioners' who 'served the occupiers . . . in Lithuania and outside its borders' is an understated acknowledgement of the extent to which local militias not only helped in the destruction of their 'own' Jewish communities but subsequently served in firing squads and death camps all over eastern Europe. No wonder, then, that many Jews of Lithuanian origin now feel towards that country and its people a peculiarly intense and intimate bitterness which no *post-hoc* (or *post-mortem*) declaration will ever do anything to assuage. Yet it also remains true that the killings began in Lithuania only with the arrival of the Nazi armies and ceased after they were finally driven back into Germany.

It should be said too that the new republic's record is better in certain respects than that of some others. Think of Austria, for example: a country, far wealthier and more populous than Lithuania, which for many decades claimed that since it had been 'occupied' by an invading German army it was itself just another of the many victims of Nazism, and therefore had no moral or physical reparations to make to anyone. Whereas the fact is that the *Anschluss* in 1936 was enthusiastically welcomed by the overwhelming majority of Austrians, who thereafter rushed to join the party and SS in disproportionate numbers. Thus they were well positioned to play a key role in the overall planning and execution of all the crimes which followed: not the least among these being the organization and close supervision of the deeds carried out by their Lithuanian, Latvian and Ukrainian auxiliaries.

Not long ago I saw on Austrian television a programme about the *Anschluss*. It began with the hysterical adulation which greeted Hitler when he drove into Vienna; and then pressed through to all the horrors that followed, the concentration camps and their countless deaths included. Naturally, the privations endured and the casualties suffered by Austrian members of the Wehrmacht on the eastern front were displayed too, as were the effects of Allied bombing raids on Austrian cities. To none of that could any fair-minded person take exception. At the end of the programme, however, a portentous voice summed up, as such voices do, the lesson of what had been shown. Over a photograph of emaciated Austrian prisoners of war on their return from Siberia several years after the end of hostilities, the voice intoned, 'Never before had a generation inflicted so much suffering on others – and suffered so much itself.'

Oh, so it all worked out fair and square in the end, did it? A little earlier in the programme a neatly dressed, grey-haired old lady had complained bitterly about Hitler's 'betrayal' of the 'idealism' of people like herself who had been young in the 1930s. So now we know. Nothing like throwing one's political opponents into concentration camps, burning books, corrupting the sciences, glorifying war, driving into silence or out of the country dissenting teachers and writers, endlessly preaching hatred of and contempt for the non-Germanic mass of mankind, and of course relentlessly tormenting and persecuting the Jews – nothing like that, was there, or is there, to bring out the 'idealism' of young people?

[17]

We approached Varniai from the south, at speed, the car radio playing hits from the 1970s. A large lake abuts on the south-east side of the town, and the countryside around it is flat even by Lithuanian standards. Thinly wooded too. Even the individual trees were skimpier and more weedy-looking than those we had seen elsewhere. There are relatively few cultivated fields nearby; instead stretches of barren-looking marshland, covered in an unpalatably reed-like growth, obtrude on the plain.

Earlier, seeing the first road signs pointing to Varniai, I had felt a strange nervousness, as if the closer I came to it in reality, the more it removed itself in my mind, and not the other way around. For years its old name, Vorna, had been a sound only; then, dressed up in its new garb as Varniai, I had seen it on a large-scale map supplied to me by the Lithuanian consulate in London; now it was a destination, with our distance from it marked in kilometres. Still the car went on. We were travelling directly north. More signs, more empty crossroads, plenty of cottages and ploughed fields. No other vehicles. Here was a turning from the road and just a few minutes later another sign on which Varniai figured at last not as a destination, not as a direction, but simply as a declaration. This was it.

My nervousness left me; or rather, it was replaced by a

misgiving different in nature. What threatened me now was anticlimax merely. Discovering that I had come here for nothing.

Albertis stopped the car, at my request. To one side was a dusty, stony space, a kind of parking lot, with some boarded-up kiosks scattered about on it. The largest of these structures – roofed in iron, built of the familiar, sand-coloured brick – looked like a garage, though it had no sign announcing it as such. It too was closed. Several hoseless, rusting petrol pumps stood nearby; another, more modern in design and in better condition, had its hose padlocked securely to itself, like a prisoner in manacles. Three or four cars waited in front of it. Their drivers and passengers were standing about in the warm sunlight, talking to one another. Presumably they were expecting the garage attendant to arrive; or, it occurred to me later, this was the place where the inter-town buses halted, and they were waiting to pick up friends or to see them off.

No one took any notice of our arrival. Everything was flat and nondescript, as if specially arranged so, for my benefit. There were some telephone poles and wires; a single no-parking sign; across the road a field of newly cut grass; further off an anonymous brick-built public building, too large for a house, too small for a school. Welcome to Varniai. The scent of grass from the field mingled with the smell of oil and dust.

All right then. Having procrastinated long enough I got back into the car and we drove on. The trees that were gathered together ahead of us separated themselves to form an avenue of young limes. Bare or grassy verges gave way to neat kerbstones. Houses and small apartment blocks appeared: unplastered, unornamented places, built of the standard, sandy-looking brick; then a cluster of shops, the same; then a few older, lower, more 'picturesque' wooden houses. I remembered my mother's proud recollection that the family home had been the only two-storeyed, brick-built house in the place (even though it had been shared with the cantor). There were hundreds of such houses now. The town hall, more imposing than some we had seen on our travels, overlooked a neat plaza; it was adorned with wide steps below and a pediment above. On the far side of town a tall red-brick factory chimney rose above yet another blur of trees.

Empty of traffic, empty of people too, the main road turns right and starts to go down a steeper slope than might have been expected, considering how flat is the countryside around the town, as well as the approach to it. Now a man appears and crosses the road ahead of us, slantingly, as pedestrians do when they are confident that no approaching vehicle will trouble them. Dressed in shorts, a shirt and wellington boots, he has a plastic pail in each hand. On his head is a white handkerchief knotted at its corners. Shlomo's informant had told him that 'the last Jew in Varniai' is a woman mathematics teacher, once married to a Lithuanian, who had taught in the local high school and is now widowed and retired. Her first name, he had said, was Vera; but her surname and address were not known to him. Seeing the bucket-carrying local, therefore, Shlomo leaps out of the car and a lively conversation ensues between them. It ends with much head-shaking on both sides.

Shlomo gets back into the car telling us not to worry, never mind, for sure he will find her. 'How many women maths teachers can there be in a place like this?' he says. It is an expression of scorn, not a question. He insists that we stay on this road, though Albertis makes a tentative dart to left or right at each crossing we come to. (There are few enough of them.) A car overtakes us and comes to a halt in response to Shlomo's frantic hand-waving through the open window. He gets out. More urgent conversation follows. Another failure.

In front of us now is a large white church. Its tower, decorated with tall, narrow, lancet-like windows, has an awkward appearance, like a man with elevated shoulders and a too-small head.

In this case the head is a silver dome in the shape of an angular onion, if such a vegetable can be imagined. It is a common architectural motif in these parts. The building was formerly a 'cloister', I will be told later: by which I assume a monastery or convent is meant. It stands on a corner, just at the point where the downhill slope flattens out and the road begins to wind up once more. Albertis brings the car to a halt. My son spots a young couple emerging from one of the houses behind us. Shlomo immediately goes scrambling after them. He points inquiringly in one direction, they point in another. An adolescent boy with a bicycle joins in the debate. So does a dog. I get out of the car and take a road going off to the left, towards what I guess must be the centre of town.

A modest bridge carries me over a stream hitherto hidden behind trees and houses. Next to the bridge stands a smaller, red-roofed church, surmounted by a delicate cross. The two churches are 100 yards apart, at most. There are wooden houses on both sides of the stream, with pathways and vegetable gardens going down in uneven steps from their back doors to the water. Upstream of the bridge a woman is doing her laundry on the river bank. Two little girls are paddling close by her, not venturing away from the rocks she stands on. They shout and giggle demonstratively, covering up their timidity with much noise. Downstream a middle-aged man in striped trunks is carefully wetting his torso before stepping into the water. Every handful of water he throws on himself shines briefly, like a necklace, in mid-air. It also produces a wide gaping of his mouth, but he is too far away for me to hear his gasps or cries. Behind him another man kneels to dig out weeds from a vegetable bed. Bells chime persistently from a church somewhere out of sight. Since both the churches I can see are closed and silent, I assume that a wedding is being celebrated elsewhere.

So this is the place.

I had wanted to be here physically, to become a part bodily

of the locale in which my grandparents spent most of their adult lives; where my mother had passed her entire childhood. I had wanted to see, touch, smell, hear what had been to them as intimate, and as much taken for granted, as Kimberley had once been to me.

Here it is. This.

The river ran for them just where it runs now, over the same rocks, making the same noise and producing the same never-ceasing swirls and bubbles on its surface. The two churches stood then where they stand now. The wooden houses set unevenly on both sides of the slope, nearer or further from the stream, cannot be those my mother saw in her childhood – they are too new and neat – but I have no doubt they are built in the style of the ones they replaced. The vegetables and flowers of late June were the same then as they are now. So is the dark, turned-over earth of a bed that awaits planting. So are the clumps of grass in neglected corners, and the white-flowering bindweed clambering up walls and tree trunks wherever it is allowed to do so. The trees carry small green apples now just as they did then. Excited little girls have always cried out like these.

No one else has appeared on the road. No car comes down it. I become aware belatedly that the chimes have stopped. My son stands on the corner by the white-towered church, waving to me to come back.

By chance Albertis had stopped the car just yards away from Vera's house, which is sited diagonally across the road from the 'cloister'. This Shlomo had learned from a neighbour. So there is Vera, the last Jew in Varniai, labouring down the road towards me, as I go up towards her. Her legs and arms are swollen; even her hands are puffed out. Her wrists are deep clefts above them. The word that occurs to me as I go towards her is 'dropsy', though I have no idea if it is one that doctors still use. She walks with difficulty. Each pace carries her forward only a little, despite the effort she puts into it. Her shoes are flattened by the weight they have to carry.

But what a fine face! Such a vivacious one too! She has wide, brown, light-filled eyes; thick hair, black and grey in colour, combed to one side and falling over her broad forehead in a single wave; narrow, slantly smiling lips; a pointed chin; many deep lines around her mouth; strong cheekbones; a neck which is still sturdy. Every averted glance or sudden, direct gaze expresses alertness, curiosity, humour; so does every tilt of her head.

All this I saw fully not so much outside her house, when we were introduced to each other, but later, at the Jewish cemetery of Varniai. For the moment I am conscious chiefly of her delight that a carload of strangers has come to visit her on an empty Saturday afternoon. She makes no attempt to hide her pleasure from us. Why should she? She has nothing to lose – nothing that we can take from her, anyway – and little to expect. Yet the curiosity and responsiveness that is in her cannot be denied.

Her house – a wooden one, with two storeys – has a tiny garden, placed sideways to the road, in which she grows peonies and tulips. She disappears through the front door, leaving us in the roadway. When she emerges I see that she has used the few moments indoors to give her hair a brisk brush and to put on some lipstick. But she has not changed the dress she is wearing, with its red and white roses all over and its floppy, V-shaped neck. I do not know what passed between her and Shlomo (who is proud and relieved to have found her) while I was standing on the bridge, out of sight; I do not even know where we are headed when she manages to heave herself into the car and Albertis starts driving back the way we had come. Before reaching the outskirts of town, however, she instructs him to turn left. The road now goes winding up a gentle incline: once again Varniai is showing me that it has more slopes than I had thought, on first seeing it couched among the flat fields, beside its dark lake.

At Vera's command the car stops at another wooden house, more meagre-looking than her own. We now learn that Vera is *not* the last Jew in Varniai. There is another woman, younger than herself, also married to a Lithuanian, who shares that solemn title with her. Vera has decided that she too is entitled to share in the excitement of our arrival.

The other last Jew in town is called Tsippele. Poorer than Vera, smaller, thinner, dressed in a pink, befrilled apron, her skimpy hair dyed the colour of iodine, she has a bony nose, light-coloured eyes and an ingratiating, half-hysterical manner.

The paintwork on the shingles of her cottage is so faded it is impossible to tell what colour they had once been; its back yard is littered with bits of machinery, boxes, buckets, cans, a dead motorbike, several live chickens, a few patches of oil. A silent man of about the same age as Tsippele, possibly her husband, but nameless, never introduced to us, stands in the doorway of a rickety shed, scrutinizing us but offering no greeting and making no movement towards us. Tsippele runs back and forth, incapable of letting us go yet barred from joining in the expedition we are about to make. There is simply no room for a sixth person in the car, so Albertis, as its owner and driver, gets it in the neck from her especially. Convinced that if she lets us go we will not return and she will never see us again, she complains, half-sobs, gesticulates and makes implausible suggestions – among them that my son should remain behind with her, as a kind of hostage, a flesh and blood guarantor of our intention to return.

Propelled by her vehemence and anxiety, we retreat from the yard and again find ourselves on the unmade road in front of the cottage. Houses like hers are scattered along lanes and double tracks that meander off at random. A wood stack, more than head-high and shaped like a tepee, stands on a piece of open ground. There are carefully tended vegetable gardens everywhere one looks. Each is laid out in a different pattern from every other; so together they make up a patchwork pattern that is larger still. In the distance rises yet another of the red-brick chimneys, taller than any of the buildings around it, in which towns like these seem to specialize.

In the end it is arranged that we will return to Tsippele's house for coffee. Clutching the wrist of each of us in turn, in order to extract successive, individual promises to that effect, she finally allows us to get into the car. Even then, pausing only to lean momentarily against the wall of her cottage and catch her breath, she still twitches and flutters about us like the bird after which she is named, before rushing into the middle of the road to give Albertis another earful and, at last, to wave goodbye.

It is not a long drive from her house to the Jewish cemetery. Inside it we find two elderly men wielding long-handled scythes near the gate. Both are tall and thin. One is wearing a hat of unusual shape and pale colour; it looks traditional and peasant-like, but turns out to carry an advertisement for INPAG (whatever that may be). Vera tells us that an American Jew whose family was originally from Varniai had visited the town two years before and had succeeded in finding his grandfather's grave in the cemetery. Subsequently he sent her money for the upkeep of the place. The mayor of Varniai has also been generous in helping her to get it in order. The first job undertaken was to erect the memorial of pink, mottled granite which stands near the entrance. A steel-stranded fence had also been put around the entire plot, with gate to match. Some of the stones have been reset (though many look too far gone ever to stand again; time has virtually driven them underground, like the bodies they had been put there to mark). Now the whole area is being cleared of grass, so that it will be easier to walk about in it.

Proud of the bargain she has driven with them, Vera tells us that she is not giving the labourers money for the job they are doing. The sole payment offered them is the grass they are cutting, which they will take home for their cows. She admits that dealing with the trees – self-seeded sycamore and ash mostly, some of them large and clustered thickly together – is going to be more of a problem, however.

The granite memorial near the gate carries a strange message; one which is unlike those on the stones of similar size and shape at the 'mass massacre' sites. Below the Star of David appear the following words in Yiddish and Lithuanian: UNTIL 1941 IN THIS PLACE [*OYF DEM ORT*] THERE USED TO BE [*IZ GEWEZEN*] THE JEWISH CEMETERY OF VARNIAI. I have to consider the wording carefully before I come to understand it. In effect, this memorial now serves as a gravestone for nothing less than the cemetery itself. Here, the inscription is telling us, where so many of the dead have lain for so many generations, my grandfather among them, there *had* been a cemetery once. Though they lie here still, it is not to be described as 'the Jewish cemetery of Varniai' now. It had ceased to be that in 1941, when the community which it 'used to' serve was destroyed.

In 1941 the people who should have been buried here went to their deaths anonymously, indiscriminately, and were thrown into the common pits and pyres which their killers had made them prepare beforehand.

Since then – no one. That is why it is a cemetery no longer.

I spent some time on my own, looking among the gravestones in the cleared section to see if I could find any bearing the names Segal or Melamed. I found none. The section which the men had cleared, nearest to the gate, was also the 'newest'; the dates of the stones in it were all post-1920s – i.e. after my grandfather's death and the departure of the family from Varniai. With an eerie exactitude, not a single stone among them was dated later than May 1941. (The job of translating the dates from the Hebrew calendar was done for me by Shlomo.) A month later the Germans invaded. June. As it is now.

Then, on my own, I wandered further afield. It would have taken all day, several days more likely, to search thoroughly through the rest of the cemetery. The uncut grass was taller than many of the stones, and so thick that nowhere did the soles of my shoes touch the earth: only grass, and last year's grass matted beneath it. Wild flowers also grew thickly everywhere: cow parsley with crunchy stalks and tiny, lace-like petals; the perfect white wheels of starworts; galaxies of shining dandelion globes. Shoes wet with dew and sap, nostrils filled with the sweetness my footsteps released from the growth they were crushing, I walked this way and that, sometimes stumbling over the uneven surface. Plenty of Rivkas, Shmuels, Avrahams, Feiges, Zalmans, Sarahs, Lezars, with surnames to match. Plenty of bright sun and trembling leaf shadows; tree trunks like columns, some seamed, some smooth; a distant view of the cloister's silver onion dome. Still no Melamed. No Segal. No Yisrael Yehoshua (Heshel).

Back in the cleared section I came on a stone which said of the sixteen-year-old boy (*bachur*) lying beneath it that he had been charming and cultured (*nechmad u-maskil*). How his parents and family must have mourned for him when he died in 1936, knowing nothing of what he was to be spared. When I translated this stone for my son, who had joined me there, he said, 'So these are the lucky ones; they were allowed a natural death.' Then he went back to Vera and Shlomo. The two Lithuanian workers were standing with Albertis at the gate, conversing in soft voices. They had laid their scythes, not irreverently I felt, against the big memorial stone near the gate. Looking back at them, and at the implements, and at the cut grass at their feet, it occurred to me that hunting for my grandfather's grave was like searching for a needle in what would soon become a haystack.

How I would have felt if I had found his stone there, among the many others, is something I cannot guess at. I do know, though, that my failure to do so did not dishearten or disappoint me. On the contrary. I had come close enough to it, and to him. He was where he belonged, hidden among the remains of the people who for centuries had preceded him and of those who had followed him: the last to have been allowed to take their place alongside him, in named, individual graves. He himself had accompanied many of the families of the dead to this spot, and had led the last prayers for them here.

Everything around me would have been familiar to him. Everything except for the memorial near the gate, with its terrible message.

I went back to Vera. 'You see,' she greeted me in Yiddish, gesturing ironically to the silent congregation around her, 'I am the *rebbitzen* of Varniai now.'

The rabbi's wife. The first lady of Varniai. The claim fell strangely on my ears, for my grandmother, Menuchah, had been wife of the *real* rabbi of Varniai, the man whose stone I had just been looking for. In his day the town's Jewish community had numbered about 700 people; they had Heshel Melamed as their rabbi, and a synagogue, and two *shtiblach* (small houses of prayer), and this cemetery waiting for them all.

Now Vera remained. She represented everyone and was responsible for everything.

We stared at one another in silence. Then she asked me where I came from. For some reason I did not answer 'England', as I had said to people everywhere else. South Africa, I said. *Dorem Afrika.*

She repeated the two words doubtfully, as if not believing me. '*Dorem Afrika?*' Then: '*F'n welche dorf?*' From what town?

Before I could answer, she asked, even more doubtfully, 'Kimberley?'

I have never in my life been so surprised at anything said to me by a complete stranger. I could only gape at her. If she had said 'Johannesburg?' or 'Cape Town?' or even 'Durban?' the effect would obviously not have been the same. People know of such places. They are big cities. But Kimberley! Here! It was as if the years I had lived and the distances I had crossed had been transformed into a single sound from her mouth, or into an object no bigger than a chip of stone or a leaf which she had effortlessly passed over to me. Here I was, in my mother's small, lost, mythical home town, which she had left eighty years before, within weeks of her father's burial in this very spot. She had never returned to it, never corresponded with anyone who remained here. Yet the first name that comes from the mouth of this woman, whom I have barely spoken to, whom I have met just minutes before, is precisely that of the small, lost, mythical town on the other side of the globe to which my mother had moved; the town I had grown up in and had also long since abandoned.

Soon, however, surprise contended with another feeling, not contradicting it, but complementing it, infusing it with a strange calm and naturalness. What could be more appropriate? What else had I come for? She is the last Jew in Varniai. I am the first person to have visited it from South Africa. (She was to confirm this later, but I knew it already, from the wondering, disbelieving tone in which she had repeated after me the syllables '*Dorem Afrika?*') Naturally, as if in a fairy story, she immediately sends me straight back to the very corner of it I still feel to be most deeply my own.

Before any of these words had passed between us, and to make their impact even stronger than they might otherwise have been, our eyes had already met in a prolonged, searching gaze: this while Shlomo was insisting that it was my duty to continue hunting for my grandfather's grave among the stones. Neither of us interrupted him, nor did we say anything to each other. We simply stared at each other with an intimacy I would hardly have thought possible between two people who had never met before. It was the kind of gaze that people might exchange in some extreme situation: like love, or illness, or pleasure, or when pleading for help. I was conscious of her wide brown eyes; the line of her eyebrows and the cleft between them; her lips curved in a reserved, speculative smile. Also of the open neck of her dress. She knew how strange it was for me to be there; also that I did not want to be told by Shlomo or anyone else how to behave.

So we stared at one another. She was the first to lower her lids, not in embarrassment, but as if to say: enough, this isn't a competition, there is no call for us to try and stare one another down. There was something else in that movement of her eyes, with its firm but courteous mingling of submissiveness and rebuke. Call it love, from another life, the life neither of us would ever lead.

The leaves moved overhead and their shadows moved too. The uncut grass swayed to its own rhythm. Albertis and the grass-cutters were squatting now, and the breeze carried the thin tang of the cigarettes they had lit.

Naturally I now wanted to know why she had asked if I came from Kimberley. She explained that she had family there. Had I known someone in Kimberley by the name of Julius Shles?

Of course. Decades before he had owned Shles's Silk Store in Jones Street. As distinct as it was distant (it was so long since I had last thought of him), his image came before my mind's eye: here, of all places, in what 'used to be' the cemetery of Varniai. I saw his grey, waistcoated suit, his stiff shoulders and flat-featured face: the face of a man who did not expect the world to do him many favours.

You see, she went on, her grandmother had been a Shles. So Julius Shles was her cousin once removed. After the war she wrote to an *organizatsya* in South Africa, asking for help in tracing her relatives there, and as a result she was put in touch with Julius Shles. He had been very good to her. In those days the Soviet government allowed people from abroad to send bolts of cloth to their relatives. She received parcels of cloth regularly from him, three or four times a year, which she would sell to others. Without his help she would never have been able to study at the university in Klaipeda. That was how she paid for the fees and managed to have enough left over to eat (*zu essen*). So in the end she was able to graduate.

Did I know his sons, Eli and Hymie? Yes, I answered, of course I did. Had she heard, it was my turn to ask, that Hymie was dead? Yes, she knew; she still received letters sometimes, seldom, from Eli. She had other relatives in the United States, but they never wrote to her. They did not want to know how hard life was for people like her (*bei uns*).

She had come to Varniai only after the war. She'd grown up in – a name I did not catch – about thirty kilometres away. After graduating she got married and some years later came to Varniai, when she was appointed to teach maths in the high school. She had done that for many years; now she was retired. (Later she said to my son, who was airing before her the many phrases of Lithuanian he had already picked up, 'Ha! I'd like to have had *you* for a pupil!')

And how – the inevitable question – had she escaped during the war? Well, it was like this. The Germans gathered maybe 2,000 women and children near Zarenai (?) to the north. The night she arrived there some of them, a big group, managed to run away (*ontloffen*). She was among them. The women and children who remained behind were shot in the woods (*im walden*) the next day. She did not know how many of the other runaways survived. She was recaptured and sent to the ghetto in Siauliai, and afterwards to the concentration camp at Stutthof. The men from her own town, from Varniai and from several other places in the neighbourhood were taken to Telz and shot there. This separation of the men and the women, and their murder in different places (*orte*), was unusual, she said, but it did sometimes happen.

Of the fate of her parents, and of brothers or sisters she might have had, I did not ask and she did not speak.

Back to Tsippele, whose promise of 'coffee' has turned in our absence into a copious, Russian-type spread of salami, smoked eel, herring, tomatoes, onions, gherkins, rye bread, cheese, jam, butter, home-made apple and raspberry wine (strong and sweet), instant coffee. And an east European speciality which I had seen and quailed at once before, consisting of a slice of pure white pork fat with a thin streak of claret-coloured meat across the top of it.

Vera sits on a couch; the rest of us, much squashed together, on chairs. In addition to the table we are sitting at, the room contains a television set, a sideboard with mirror, a glass-fronted, glass-shelved cupboard revealing a variety of jugs, tumblers, wine glasses and bowls within, and a large wood-burning stove (shut down for the summer) with a tiled chimney going all the way to the ceiling. On top of the cupboard is a large, rectangular clock in a wooden case (stopped), with a similar but smaller rectangular clock perched on it (working). Other items in view include a cluster of no less than three wooden crucifixes of different sizes affixed to a wall, a trunk resting on the floor, an ambitious rubber plant and a pair of photographs in matching plastic frames. There is no door between this room and the equally cluttered, narrow kitchen beyond. Nor is there any sign of the man we had seen outside.

Tsippele jumps up and down, passes items around, insists we eat everything, eats nothing herself, refills our glasses with apple and raspberry wine, and begins to shine at the eyes and tremble at the lips as she tells us what a hard life she leads with her husband, who beats her and calls her a dirty Jewess whenever he gets drunk. To this Vera utters a stern '*Schweig!*' ('Shut up!') Also, Tsippele goes on, with every syllable getting still shinier at the eyes and more trembly at the lips, she is poor, she has no money at all, her husband gives her nothing. (Vera: '*Schweig! Schweig!*') At this reprimand Tsippele blubs a bit, but schweigs, and soon the two women have begun making jokes about the pork and the eel on the table. Vera says to me, 'I told you I'm the *rebbitzen* of Varniai, so if I say it's kosher, then it's kosher.' She tucks into it all with great appetite, pork, fish, cheese, whatever is put in front of her; indeed she is still eating when everybody else, myself, my son, Shlomo, even the thin, ever-hungry Albertis, is finished. We all do well, but Vera outdoes us all.

Over the meal I learn that Tsippele was born in Varniai. She survived the war because a Catholic priest took her mother, herself and her two sisters under his protection. (She says nothing about her father.) The priest succeeded in settling them in different peasant families in the countryside, where they grew up. She was five years old when the Germans came. So she was born in 1936, almost twenty years after my grandfather's death. When I ask (not expecting a positive answer) if she remembers anyone in the town ever mentioning to her a family Melamed, she admits that the name means nothing to her. And Segal? After much frowning and many nervous, self-coaxing nods of the head, she says that she *thinks* she once heard of such a family living there. But even if she is telling the truth, and not merely trying to be obliging (I suspect the latter), how likely is it that 'her' Segals have anything to do with my grandfather's previous existence under that name?

So I ask another question. Does she remember where the rabbi used to live?

How she would love to answer me affirmatively! But, to her credit, she cannot do so. Torn between the wish to please and the fear of letting herself into a labyrinth of untruths, she remains dumb, capable only of casting beseeching looks in Vera's direction. Replete yet attentive, Vera remains magisterially aloof. She makes no response whatever.

Time to go. In the pathway between the side entrance to the house and the road I give Tsippele *a kleine matonneh*: about forty litas ($10). She bursts into tears again. Presses wet kisses on my cheek. Clutches me by the hand, the neck, the shoulder, the waist. Insists on my son taking photographs of us all. Shows a bossy streak in organizing where and in what order we should stand. At every crucial photographic moment she sends a hand stealing over my shoulder. Earlier, in the house, when Albertis had taken a picture of the supper party, she had made him wait while she went to the mirror in the sideboard and combed her pitifully thin, iodine-coloured locks.

It is alarming to see Vera labour up the steep, slippery, wooden stairs that lead to her rooms on the upper floor of her house. But she makes it, eventually. It appears that she occupies that floor (or a part of it) only. Her rooms are small but positively middle class or schoolmistressly compared with Tsippele's. She leads us into a little study, with desk, chairs and a spare bed. Her books are neatly ranged on shelves; among them is a Lithuanian encyclopedia in many volumes. Framed diplomas and photos hang on the walls. Out of a leatherette folder stuffed with papers she takes the visiting card of the American Jewish benefactor who has sent her money for the upkeep of the cemetery. His name is Davis; he comes from Chicago; he describes himself as the Administrator of Mid-American Convalescent Centers. She also shows me cards she has kept from the two other people from the United States who called on her when they visited Varniai. I give her some money as my contribution to the fund for the cemetery; also an additional sum which I tell her is for herself. She accepts it gratefully, but it puts her on her mettle. She must give us a present in return. From one of the drawers in the desk she takes out another folder. Do we collect stamps? My son gallantly says that he does. So she starts picking out unused, special-issue stamps from that folder: some of this kind, some of that, more of others. She puts more and more into an envelope before we are able to persuade her to desist.

This potlatch-like exchange completed, I learn that she has one son in Vilnius, one in Kaunas and a granddaughter studying English and German at the university in Klaipeda. She had been hoping that the son in Kaunas would be visiting her this weekend, but he is busy playing bridge – in a big tournament, she adds, a mixture of pride and scorn in her voice. Whether the scorn is directed against him (for choosing to play bridge instead of coming to see her) or against herself (for being proud of his success at the game), I cannot determine. He, the bridge player, is her 'Jewish' son, she says, with a brief, enigmatic smile. Then she explains what she means by this, if not what she feels about it. 'He is dark.' (*Er iz tunkel.*)

I ask her what she knows about pre-war Varniai. She sighs, shakes her head, sits in silence. She hadn't lived here then. All she knows about pre-war Varniai is that it was gone by the time she arrived. It had been destroyed. A battle was fought across it in '41; and then another, fiercer battle during the German retreat in '44. Everything was levelled, except for a few of the bigger buildings, like the churches. They too were badly damaged. After the war the whole town was rebuilt. The streets no longer run where they used to. Who can say where exactly anything was?

So, like the site of my grandfather's grave, the whereabouts of his house and *shul* remain hidden from me. Should I hunt for them further? From whom? Some aged gentile in the town whose memories would be no clearer or more reliable than Tsippele's? And to what end? I find a shrinking in myself from the prospect of hunting around the town and eventually gazing at a street of unplastered brick houses like all the others; or some little apartment block, or group of shops, or clinic, or set of school buildings. More, in short, of the kind of thing we had seen as we came in, and are to see yet again as, at my request, we take a different route out of town.

Besides, even if Varniai has been wholly rebuilt since the war, I am certain that I have seen something – the cemetery aside – that cannot have changed since my grandfather lived here and my mother was a child; indeed, that could not have changed for centuries before that too. The route we had followed coming into the town, with the downward curve of the road paralleling the course of the river, and then being crossed by the road I had walked along, to where the bridge now stands, and where there had obviously once been a ford – these topographical features are now what they always have been. They had determined the direction of the tracks made by the first people to gather at the site, however many hundreds or even thousands of years before. Around them the town had risen. They, and the lake to the west, had given it its shape. They do so still.

We get up to leave. Vera follows us downstairs. Big hugs and kisses follow. Saying goodbye to her, I remember the Yiddish word *edel* which my parents sometimes used about people they admired. Its origin is the German *edel* (noble), but there is nothing feudal and aristocratic about the Yiddish use of it. In Yiddish it refers to decency, honesty, refinement of feeling.

A few things still have to be said about my meeting with Vera.

The first I could have mentioned to her at the time, if only I had remembered it. My uncle Leib, oldest son of the one-time rabbi of Varniai, passer-on to me in wretched circumstances of his grandfather's BOOK, had been employed for many years by the South African Jewish Board of Deputies in Johannesburg. As head of its social welfare department he was given the responsibility, immediately after the war, of setting up a bureau to help survivors of the Holocaust get in touch with members of their families in South Africa – and vice versa. (Vera's *organizatsya*, in other words.) Her name and Julius Shles's must have passed under his gaze, though it is inconceivable he would have noticed them, among the thousands of others. Especially as the name Varniai would not have appeared next to either of them, as it was not from there that they had come.

Also: since meeting her I have done some reading about the Stutthof concentration camp, to which she was sent after her time in the ghetto of Siauliai. I had not heard of Stutthof before meeting her; or at any rate had no recollection of doing so. It was sited in Poland, twenty miles east of Danzig (Gdansk); and all I shall say about it here is that mass killings, elaborate forms of torture and enforced 'evacuations' went on unabated there until 15 April 1945. That is, until three weeks before the formal surrender of the German forces everywhere in Europe.

Finally, this. In a recent letter Vera wrote to me (in German), 'You are my brother.'

[18]

The last Jew in Kelme, Berelis by name, is a plump, tragic-faced, Assyrian figure with a black beard, an arched nose, flared nostrils and a direct brown stare. He wears a gaudy short-sleeved sports shirt decorated with flowers and spear-like leaves. With every breath he takes his broad chest expands and his shoulders rise slowly, before he expels abruptly the air he has just drawn in. The process is so laborious it seems to take far more out of him than he gets from it. His manner suggests that he accepts reluctantly the role of the person in Kelme to whom all inquiring Jewish visitors from abroad are bound to come. He is a doctor, a public servant, a responsible man in early middle age; but he strikes me as more obviously death-haunted than either Vera or Tsippele, who were alive at the time of the catastrophe. There are no jokes from him about his being the 'rabbi' of Kelme. Nor do I have the impression that he has any interest in me and my son, of the kind that Vera had shown. Individual temperament aside, visitors from abroad are clearly at far less of a premium here in Kelme, since it is so much bigger a town than Varniai, and was once so much more important a centre of Jewish life and learning.

However, having met us outside his big, solidly built house, he courteously invites us into it and leads the way up the tiled steps to the front door. I notice that when we have passed through the door he takes care to lock it behind us. We go into a big central chamber, more like a hall than a living room, with a flight of stairs going up on one side to the floor above. For all its size the room looks over-furnished, though in a greatly different style from Tsippele's; it abounds in heavily stuffed settees and armchairs, wooden chests and sideboards, large and small tables, gaudy pictures, bright rugs (on the floor and on the walls), fringed runners, flowers made of straw, dados carrying plates and other knick-knacks. All the wooden surfaces, banisters included, shine as if many layers of varnish have been spread on them.

At the far end of the room an elderly man is sitting by himself, watching on television yet another of the football games in the current European Nations' tournament. He nods to us, but no introductions are made. We are taken through a side door into Berelis's study or consulting room. My son and I sit on a swollen sofa, Berelis in an armchair opposite. A low glass-topped coffee table stands between us. We learn that the man watching television is his father-in-law. Just as we had with Vera in Varniai, we learn once again that Berelis is not *quite* the last Jew in Kelme; his father-in-law shares that distinction with him. He, the father-in-law, had married a Lithuanian woman, who has since died. So, Berelis says, of the 2,000 Jews who used to live here, there are now two. (*F'n zwei toizent bleibt noch – zwei.*) He holds up his index and middle fingers, together, so that I can see just what that means.

Minutes later Berelis's wife, who is to my eye wholly Lithuanian in appearance, and their daughter, a thin, dark-haired girl in her late teens, come in separately. The one brings a bowl of fruit, the other plates and knives for us to use in eating the fruit; both withdraw almost immediately.

By that time Berelis has produced a folder of papers and a book about the destruction of the Jews of Kelme. Almost every

movement he makes is accompanied by a deep heave for breath.
It is not a sigh: his manner is not at all lugubrious – it is driven,
rather, even angry. Peremptorily, like a man who has done this
often before, he asks me in Yiddish: who were my people?
(Earlier he had shaken his head dismissively when Shlomo, who
was also meeting him for the first time, had said to me, '*He'll*
be able to speak to you in English' – an expression of misplaced
confidence which clearly sprang from Shlomo's esteem for Berelis's status as a doctor and professional man.) I answer by saying
that the names I am especially interested in are Oppenheim and
Beinashowitz. My great-grandfather, Zvi Yakov Oppenheim,
had served as rabbi of the biggest of Kelme's synagogues and
as head of the local rabbinical council. On his death he was
succeeded in both posts by his son-in-law, Beinashowitz, who
was married to my great-aunt Rachel. Another of Zvi Yakov's
daughters (Merre) and a son (Bendor) were also living in the
town when the Germans took it in 1941. Merre, who was
divorced from her husband, had two sons. I do not know
whether or not Bendor had children.

Berelis listens intently, then passes over to me the book he
has been holding in his hand. It has blue covers and is published
by the Tel Aviv University Press; its text is in Hebrew; its title
is *Kelm – Etz Karut*. I know that the word '*etz*' means a tree,
and I assume (rightly, as it turns out) that '*karut*' must mean
felled, amputated, destroyed. Berelis tells me that he helped to
compile the book, though his name appears nowhere on it;
evidently he feels a certain disappointment on that score. At
the back of the book is a collection of photographs; perhaps
twenty pages of them, some with as many as six or eight
passport-sized pictures on them. All are men, if I remember
rightly. I look at the pictures and read the Hebrew names
beneath them. One page, another, another.

There he is, Kalman Beinashowitz, on the page: a thin-faced
man, sparsely bearded, his head turned slightly to one side. He

wears a tall silk skullcap; his expression is melancholy; his eyes and his chin are tilted downwards, not so much out of modesty, it seems, as out of an habitual reticence or withdrawal.

I show the picture to Berelis. 'He was married to my grandmother's sister.'

A shrug. A heave for breath. A flare of the nostrils. Eyes intent on me yet hardly seeing me. He opens his plump hands in a gesture of despair which, with a turn of the wrist, becomes one of inquiry. Anyone else?

But I linger for a moment over Kalman's thin, pensive face. He and his wife, Rachel, were childless. That item of information about them had been passed on to me by my aunt Sadie many years before, in the days of an apparently immovable Soviet occupation of the country, when neither of us had dreamt that one day I would be able to go there, to sit in a house in Kelme, to look through this gallery of portraits and to find his picture among them. Knowing how passionate is the commitment of all pious Jews to family life, as an idea and a reality, I am sure that to him and his wife their childlessness must have been a source of much grief. Now, with this book in my hand, I wonder if they did not think of it as a bitter blessing to them both, when the time of terror came? As a source of dark comfort?

I look further through the book. No Oppenheims appear. The married name of the other daughter, Merre, is not known to me. Though they were called 'the boys' by the family in South Africa, her two sons must have been about thirty years old when the Germans arrived. They may well be among the younger of the men whose photographs are bunched together at the back. But as I have never been given a surname for them, I fall back on the notion that among all these murdered men I may be able to identify a familiar line of mouth or nose, cheek or eye socket. Familiar, I mean, in the most literal sense: belonging to the family.

Inevitably I cannot find what I am looking for. Or to speak

more truly, I see it everywhere. Any of these pairs of eyes or lips, any of these brows or beards or cheeks will do. There is not a portrait in this stark gallery that might not, will not, silently reveal a possible cousin, if I look long enough at it.

Karut, all of them, as the title of the book says: felled, amputated, destroyed.

In the meantime, Berelis has brought out from his folder a photocopy of a list of names. It too is in Hebrew, and looks like a computer print-out. It was sent to him from Israel, apparently, and contains the names of all the Jews known to have been living in Kelme in 1941. He runs a finger down the list. Ah, here. An Oppenheim. But he has difficulty reading the first name. Is it Bendov?

No, I tell him, Bendor. That's him, my great-uncle. In the family he was always known simply as Benne. He too was a rabbi; he was the one who put together the writings in his father's posthumous BOOK – the last ragged copy of which I had deposited at the Vilnius Jewish State Museum days before.

And a wife? Not listed. Children? Not listed.

Yet, so far as I know, he was a married man; and so probably a father too.

Everything is a great effort for Berelis. Under heavy lids his eyes burn with energy and a kind of manic grief. The responsibility of being the last Jew in Kelme weighs heavily on him; the sense of it seems never to leave him. It is so burdensome to him I am half-afraid, as we sit there, that he will simply find our presence too exhausting, and ask us to leave. Yet his movements are loose-jointed for a man carrying so much weight, and his eyes and turns of his head are always watchful.

We must understand the position, he says. His work leaves him no time for himself. He is exhausted. Every day he has to drive to his office in Siauliai and back. It is a long way. And he has all the rest of the district to look after too. And then there is this – and he points at the book and papers now lying on the table.

While we eat our apples he peruses the list further, turning over one page after another. No more Oppenheims or Beinashow-itzes appear. He tells me that, like Varniai, Kelme was virtually razed to the ground during the war. Fighting took place in it and around it during both the German advance and retreat. The synagogues were burnt down; nothing remains of them. Barely any houses are left from that time. Almost word for word I hear from him what I had been told earlier in Varniai: even the streets, he says, no longer run where they used to.

Which reminds him to bring out a map of a reconstruction of Kelme that had been made from old records (I am not sure whether in Israel or the United States). Here was the great *shul* (where Zvi Yakov and Kalman Beinashowitz had in turn presided); here across the corner from it was a *yeshiva*; here, next to the *yeshiva*, another, smaller *shul*. Jews lived all over the town, but especially in these streets nearby. He looks at his watch. Come, he'll show us where they were.

We get into his car. I expect him to stop in the centre of the town, to show us the locality he had just spoken of, but he goes straight through it. We head westwards first, then north. The town peters out. We drive along a minor road before halting at a fenced-off place to the left. The fence marks off a plot of ground big enough, perhaps, for a brief terrace of town houses to be built on it. A path runs down the middle of it. Low, cut stones, like kerbstones, divide it into four rectangular 'beds'. No flowers grow from them: they contain only pebbles, dandelions and coarsely cut grass. In the middle of the plot stands yet another of the memorial stones, polished on one side, rough-hewn around the edges, that by now have become so familiar to me. In Lithuanian and Yiddish it tells the reader that to this place the Jewish men, women and children (*inglach*) from Kelme were brought out in September 1941 and shot.

Though he must have often visited the site, Berelis has to make a bigger effort than before to draw in the deepest breath he has yet taken. Only after it has come and gone does he tell me that almost 2,000 Jews were killed here. By gunfire. The entire community from Kelme.

Everyone is silent. There is a fence on the other side of the plot; beyond it are some trees and thick, tall, green Lithuanian grass. Menuchah's brother and her two sisters and their children lie where they fell. Like all the others. Bone of my bone; DNA of my DNA.

Berelis turns. He points to a small hillock behind us and to the left, just outside the fence. A pine tree grows from it, brambles sprawl around its base. It is not twenty yards away and maybe fifteen feet at its highest. High enough to 'command' the site. It is not a difficult site to command.

He says, 'The shooters stood there.'

They stood there; the people stood here, group after group, and fell into the pits some of them had been compelled to dig earlier. Everything at point-blank range, a matter of yards only. Every shot heard all over Kelme, at a distance of less than a mile. Did they march them out in groups, I wonder, or bring out all 2,000 and have them milling about in the field directly across the little road? But that is another question I do not ask.

Back in the middle of town, Berelis halts the car. The road is a wide one. A few cars are parked on it, but none pass us. Nearby are two or three bus stops, some nondescript municipal offices and a group of humble shops. One of them has a neon sign shining in its window; several letters are missing from it but I would not understand what it says anyway. No one is sitting on the wooden benches next to the bus stops. The only people to be seen are the inevitable group of young men standing on a corner further down. We could be anywhere, in any east European town of modest size. In front of the municipal buildings is an open space with a paved walkway lined by a double row of trees. Signs show where cars may be parked, and where not.

Berelis tells us that the big *shul* used to stand just here. Just there. Like this. A circular motion of his hand seems to take in a bit of the road, the municipal offices, the space in front of them, perhaps the bus stops and benches.

Before leaving London I had seen a photograph of this *shul* in a collection of such photographs entitled *The Ruins of Lithuania: A Chronicle of the Destruction of the Sacred Jewish Communities of Lithuania, 1941–1944.* The picture showed an imposing structure, for once not at all 'Oriental' in aspect – Second Empire, if anything, like a provincial opera house – with many large windows and a pediment interrupted by three curious, shield-shaped gables. The caption to the picture read: 'The Great Synagogue (*Beth Ha-Midrash*) of Kelm'. Sharing the page on which it appeared was a reproduction of the blurry, seaweedy portrait of Zvi Yakov Oppenheim which I have already described.

Now I walk in the space where his synagogue had stood. (It was burnt down in 1941; with some members of the community, it is said, locked inside it.) Within its incinerated walls, under its absent roof, this is where Zvi Yakov had come to pray and study, and to sermonize on holy days to his congregation. Then his son-in-law did the same after him.

Looking about me, I understand something that has been haunting me since my arrival in Lithuania; that I had drawn close to in Varniai, but had failed to articulate there. It now seems to me that I should have always known it. The abyss of the past does not have to be figured for us by bottomless pits, vertiginous plunges, stones dropping for ever down soundless chambers. This will do just as well. These benches and that set of civic buildings; those trees and traffic signs; the curve of this empty road.

We turn at the corner into a narrow street with a few wooden cottages on it. Berelis says that he has managed to establish that two of them were here before the war. Of the two, that deserted one at the end, its windows and doorways boarded up, its roof and walls swathed in black tar-paper from roof-beam to foundation, as if in eternal mourning – that was definitely a Jewish house. On the doorpost (and he shows us where) you can see where the *mezuzah* has been gouged out of it.* The door itself had been taken away by someone from Cleveland, Ohio, and put in a *shul* there as a memorial to the martyrs of Kelme.

This is the third time in our conversation that Berelis, quite of his own accord, has mentioned Cleveland, my grandfather's prime destination when he went to the United States in 1912. Yet another reference to Cleveland (a long story about an umbrella) was to come later. So the connection between the Jews of Cleveland and the town of Kelme was indeed as close as I had assumed it to be, looking at my grandfather's address book.

Then we drive to the old Jewish cemetery on the other side of town. About the same distance from the centre as the massacre site, it is far larger than the cemetery in Varniai. Several acres of it are spread over a gentle slope that eventually rises high enough to cut off the view on that side. To the west you can see the town, beyond a winding river and some small meadows. To the south the cemetery is directly overlooked by one of those mysterious factories with an oversize red-brick

*A *mezuzah* is a small case, containing passages from Deuteronomy inscribed on parchment, which is affixed to the doorpost of a pious Jew's house.

chimney, with which every town in Lithuania seems to be adorned. There is an empty, broken-paved yard around it. When I ask Berelis what kind of factory it is, he surprises me by replying matter-of-factly, 'A bakery.'

Near the broken iron gate of the cemetery stands yet another large memorial stone. As with the one in Varniai, the inscription on it is in the past tense only. It states that for many hundreds of years this place served as the burial ground for the ancient Jewish community of Kelme: a town once famous, it goes on to say, for the piety of its people and the wisdom of its sages and learned men.

The gravestones themselves stand or lie deep in the grass, which grows even higher here than it had in Varniai cemetery. There is no section of the cemetery which has been cleared, as in Varniai. The grass stems are like jets rising and breaking into drops at their summit, before they fall back. These drops, though, are seeds. Growing higher still are innumerable dandelion stalks. They are the tallest and most profuse I have ever seen: thousands upon thousands of them, holding their globes erect. It has been dandelion time everywhere in Lithuania; even in the middle of Vilnius and Kaunas the air has often been suddenly filled with dandelion seeds floating down between buildings and accumulating in gutters. But nothing I have seen is comparable to this. Every step I take sets off silent, weightless explosions of seeds. They fly in all directions, even as the heavy heads of grass sink under my steps. The sun is setting and the seeds flying into its horizontal rays are as numberless – I cannot help thinking – as the souls of the dead. Shining too. Further away, where my feet have not yet disturbed them, the globes shimmer in the breeze like little lanterns.

Carved into the nearest tombstones are names exactly like those I had seen in Varniai. I wade through the grass as if through water to reach this one, that one, a third, a fourth. The dead lie for hundreds of yards in all directions around me.

Somewhere among them are the remains of my great-grandfather Zvi Yakov, and of my great-grandmother Beile; also
(I remember being told) my great-great-grandfather Michael
Yitzchak and his wife, Tsiporah. It hardly matters where. I
know where all the other Jews of Kelme are buried.

We drive back to Berelis's house and shake hands in his
driveway, where we had first met. I feel, without any sense of
rebuff, that he is not sorry to see us go.

The Lithuanian version of the inscription on the stone at the
massacre site just outside Kelme states that 483 Jews are buried
there. Berelis insisted that the number killed was actually close
to 2,000. That was the size of the community when the Germans
arrived – the pre-war census figures show it, and so do Jewish
records – and only handfuls of them were killed elsewhere or
managed to flee with the Russian army. There had been an
argument with the local authorities about the number that
should appear on the memorial. The authorities insisted on
using the smaller figure – Berelis does not know where they got
it from – and eventually he and the other Jews involved gave
way. Finally he had said to them, 'All right, you can put down
the number you want. But then you've got to give us back the
missing fifteen hundred people. Alive.'

That, I suppose, must be called a Jewish joke.

PART FOUR

Now

[19]

Time now for me to turn directly to you, my dear grandfather, and to offer you my apologies. Not mockingly or self-abasingly; but out of the shame I feel at having lived so long and understood so little about us both. Which is to say: about the world given to us to live in but never to share.

First. Because of the decision you took to go back to Varniai, instead of settling in Cleveland, Ohio, I now know that the grudge I had held against you was even deeper than I had supposed. It sprang, obviously and irrationally, from your having 'chosen' to expose yourself, your wife and your children to the hideous death that would have been your lot and theirs, had you lived to enforce your will on the family. My mother among them, inevitably.

Yes, she too. She would have been just like all the other murdered women, the many tens of thousands of them in Lithuania, the millions of them elsewhere in Europe. They *were* just like her, precisely in each dear detail that made her different from the others, and every one of them different from her – her lambent brown eyes behind rimless glasses; her plump figure; her delicate calves and ankles; her large head; her puzzled brow and mouth; her curling, silky hair which she always wore short but could never control; her readiness to believe the best about people; her absent-mindedness and ineptitude with her hands; her vulnerability to spells of disabling depression; her incapacity to tell even the most harmless social untruth; her childish amusement at certain kinds of absurdity; the excessive devotion she displayed towards her younger siblings and the striking lack of devotion with which she responded to her husband's wishes and rages. Nothing of her, none of this, would have been mourned or remembered, since all likely mourners or rememberers would have suffered the same fate as herself. You and Menuchah among them; and her brothers and sisters and the children they would have had; and the unknown husband she would doubtless have had by then; and the children she would have loved as much as those she bore in South Africa.

Of course I knew that you would have sent your children to the furthest corner of the earth rather than let them be murdered; I knew you had no notion of what was going to happen to the Jews of Europe. Who did? Who could have foreseen a future so terrible that only a madman could envisage it and believe (rightly!) that he would find people ready to turn it into a reality for him?

That much was plain to me and had always been so. Yet something – reproach, blame, resentment – remained. I had to go to Lithuania to get rid of it. In some of the recesses of my own mind I had found it easier to reproach the helpless than to confront the real villains, the murderers who came from the west.

Second. Your decision to return to Lithuania from the United States, and to remain there, was a principled one. You put your faith first. Of course the people who had asked you to join them in Cleveland wanted you there precisely because they needed your help in the task of preserving that faith. Yet the way of life you glimpsed in America seemed to you so repellent, you could not tolerate the thought of exposing yourself or your children to it. So you rejected the whole thing.

Should your descendants, then, not have honoured you for the earnestness with which you clung both to your beliefs and to the places that had sustained them for so many centuries?

Well, it did not work like that. How could it, when the stakes turned out to be so high? Along with all the others I had the advantage of knowing how suicidal your decision to return to Lithuania was, or would have been, had you lived to see it through. As a result the sense of reproach I felt did not confine itself to you alone; it spread from you to your religion. That too became irrevocably tainted in my eyes. On every account it was wrong, fatal, misguided. It was wrong factually, in being postulated on entities and events which did not exist: a purposive, intervening God, a history supposedly derived from his acts and wishes, and the prospect of a world-transforming, trans-historical redemption (the coming of the Messiah) which was never going to happen. More than that, it was morally culpable too, in that it had persuaded an entire people to keep themselves together, separate from all others. To what end? Solely to experience the endless nightmare of wandering and persecution assigned to them. Culminating in a horror that was 'trans-historical' only in being unlike anything else that history had yet witnessed.

So for heaven's sake, or for God's own sake, let go! Bring it to an end. For how much longer should this grisly performance be allowed to continue?

'The game was never worth the candle,' my uncle Leib once said to me, apropos of all Jewish history. And to one of my brothers he said, 'What did the Jews think was going to happen to them, if they carried on like that? Over there? They lay with their head in the lion's mouth and imagined that the lion would never close its jaws on them. Well, it did.'

My mother spoke less reproachfully, but to similar effect. 'Whenever I hear people talking about "the Jewish contribution to civilization",' she once said to me, 'I want to tell them that none of it was worth the life of a single child the Nazis murdered.' To this I responded, out of curiosity rather than out of a belief in what I was saying, 'Perhaps people value the life of a child as much as they do *because* of the Jewish contribution to civilization.' 'Oh,' she said, with a tartness that was not really characteristic of her, and a weary gesture of the wrist that was, 'Oh, they'd have discovered it without us.'

At least she was not postulating an 'alternative' history for the Jews, as Leib had done, and as I had been trying to do, in using the decisions you had taken, Heshel Melamed, to arraign the religion and the peoplehood underwritten by it. In effect, what I was asking of the Jews in eastern Europe was a complete reconstruction of their history and the circumstances in which they had found themselves. Which is an absurdity. In that part of the world there had never been a neutral, secular, social space from which they had chosen to exclude themselves. Most of those who were lucky enough to leave Europe in the earlier decades of the century did manage to find, and in some cases help to create, more open societies in which they could live according to their own inclinations. Those who remained in the 'ancestral' territories of the former Pale, however, continued to be what they had always been: one among a multitude of competing groups – ethno-religions, I would call them, or once-and-future nations – gasping for life and breath under a variety of contested sovereignties. I might as well have scolded the Poles for choosing to be Catholic and to live between the hammer of the Germans and the anvil of the Russians; or the Armenians for choosing to speak their own language, to worship Christ according to their own rite, and to place themselves between Orthodox Russians on one side and Turkic Muslims on the other.

It is all nonsense of course. Yet I know what drove me towards it. To the murderers of the Jews, the perpetrators of the Final Solution, I had nothing to say. Not even an oath to utter. From them my imagination could only reel back in fear and despair. So once again I turned in unspoken reproach towards the victims – for no better reason than that they were available, they were weak, I knew them, I could so easily have been one of them.

Third. I said earlier that people of my background, growing up where we did, were inclined to think of our predecessors as having come from Nowhere. In the end the Nazi occupation of eastern Europe, and of most of central and western Europe too, did horribly succeed in turning it into Nowhere, Nirgends, Nichts, as far as the Jews were concerned. They had to pay an unreckonable price for the vulnerabilities imposed on them by their own history and the history of the peoples around them. But it was not preordained that one day the Nazis should come out of the west with the intention of killing them all. They had not lived through those many previous centuries with the intention of making a prey of themselves.

On one side of the ocean, death. On the other, life. The gulf between those swallowed by the catastrophe in Europe and those who escaped it is unbridgeable. A commensurate gulf yawns between the catastrophe itself and the words I have to use in speaking of it. Even to you, Heshel Melamed. I sit here transcribing from my notebook Karl Jaeger's tally of his unit's killings on this or that day in Rasenai in August 1941. (On 18 August, for example: 446 Jews, 440 Jewish women, 1,020 Jewish children.) Those are his words and figures. And my words? They describe my own memory of Rasenai. The discomforts of the Hotel Neris. My visits to other 'mass massacre' sites. A childhood in Kimberley. The landscapes of Lithuania. Your visit to Cleveland, Ohio, in 1912. Vera, the last Jew in Varniai. The woman with her weighing machine on Gediminas Street, Vilnius.

This adjective or that? A full stop or a semicolon? The active or passive mood? Seeking and finding the answers to such questions, by instinct or calculation, I know that anyone who truly opened his imagination to just a fragment of what happened on the outskirts of Rasenai on 18 August 1941 might well be struck dumb for ever. And that was the tally of one day's killings of helpless people, most of them children, outside a single provincial town in Lithuania. Comparable events took place elsewhere in Lithuania and in many other countries on that same day. They went on unabated, every day, without pause, all over eastern Europe, for a further three and a half years.

I wonder what would have become of your faith if you had lived long enough to learn of such things, even from a distance. In Cleveland, say. Possibly, for reasons I obviously have great difficulty in understanding, they would have strengthened your attachment to the God of Israel and his mysterious purposes. That certainly seems to have been the effect they had on many other believers who survived the Holocaust and who have since helped to bring about the revival of orthodox belief and practice which is such a noticeable feature of contemporary Jewish life. The degree to which they have succeeded over the last few decades can no more be disputed than the present growth of evangelical Christian communities in the United States, or the resurgence of Islam elsewhere.

There is one difference, though, between the orthodox Jewish revival and the others I have just compared it to. The number of Muslims and Christians in the world is increasing overall; the number of Jews, by contrast, is rapidly shrinking. The decline in size of the small community in South Africa has been especially dramatic; but it is not out of line with what has been happening in countries with much bigger Jewish populations, like the United States, Canada, Great Britain and, more recently, France. Ultimately, orthodox Jewry, progenitive and highly visible though it is, amounts to not much more than a small minority within a group which, outside Israel at any rate, is itself dwindling in size.

Look at your own family. You and Menuchah had nine children. All reached adulthood. They in turn produced a total of fourteen children – not grandchildren 'for you', as people say, since you saw none of them, but after you, anyway. Twelve of those grandchildren survived their childhood; eleven are alive today. In their turn they have produced (according to the best calculation I can make) twenty-six great-grandchildren, who have themselves fathered or mothered a further ten great-great-grandchildren (so far).

Biologically speaking, these figures are unimpressive. A demographer would shake his head over them. You and Menuchah had nine children between the two of you. Yet those nine and their partners (eighteen people) between them succeeded in generating a total of only twelve offspring. Those twelve and all *their* partners (twenty-four) produced only twenty-six great-grandchildren. Compare the ratio of 2:9 (your and Menuchah's achievement) with that of 18:12 in the following generation, or of 24:26 in the generation after that, which is my own. Any statistician would conclude from these sums that your stock is in severe decline.

This breakdown will seem to you all the more depressing when I go on to say that many of the grandchildren and great-grandchildren I have just numbered can look back not only to east European Jewish but also to Afrikaner, Scottish, Scotch-Irish, English and Spanish ancestors. Of your twelve grandchildren no less than eight married 'out'. In other words, the rate of intermarriage among them has been quite as striking as the paucity of births. In terms of the Jewish law – to the interpretation and observance of which you devoted your life – at least half of them, my own children included, are not Jewish at all.

An extreme example, perhaps; but by no means an unparalleled one. Most western Jews have attained middle-class or upper-middle-class standards of life; and have a reproductive rate to match. Marriages between Jews and gentiles have for many years been commonplace in all the English-speaking countries. My own hunch also – though I know of no one who shares it, or admits to sharing it – is that the appalling memory of the Holocaust has *in itself* encouraged both manifestations just referred to: the low birth-rate and the high rate of intermarriage. This in spite of the efforts of those who believe that the martyrdom of European Jewry should remain for ever at the heart, or as the heart, of a continuing Jewish consciousness.

Things are different in Israel, you must admit. The establishment of the state was another and greatly different response to what had happened to the helpless Jews of Europe. A disappearing Jewish population is not a problem there. But never fear, I am not going to berate you for missing that boat too; for doing your best, in fact, to prevent it from ever sailing. I will just leave you to make what you can of the fact that the state did actually manage to come into existence, all the odds against it doing so notwithstanding. Also that the orthodox sections of its population now have so much influence over every area of the country's social and political life.

Prophecies about the future of the Jews, or about the fate of mankind in general, are not my business, however. The only thing I know for certain of the future which I will not live to see is that my ignorance of it is as profound as your ignorance, Heshel Melamed, was of the future you did not live to see. All of us suffer equally under history's iron law – its only law – which it enforces with an equal degree of rigour on every generation in turn. We are all revealed to those who come after us to have been ignorant by necessity, solemn prophets who knew little or nothing of what really lay ahead.

In the spirit of which remarks I offer you the following further items of information. Whether you will draw comfort from them it is impossible for me to guess. I have just spoken of the high rate of intermarriage among your grandchildren. By now all your great-grandchildren, too, are old enough to have set up homes of their own. Among their households there is one which stands out among the rest for its conscientious observance of the Jewish festivals, and their accompanying domestic rituals. It is run by a Midwestern American woman of impeccably Anglo-Saxon ancestry, who underwent a conversion to ortho-dox Judaism while living in Israel. She had visited the country out of curiosity, in the first instance; subsequently returned to it to work on a kibbutz; and then became a convert – not, as people might suppose, in order to marry your great-grandson, but simply because she wished to. Their marriage came later. Now they live in Arizona, together with their three children. I doubt if their notion of how observant Jews should live would meet your standards in such matters; nevertheless, were you to visit them, I am sure you would recognize that they are doing their best to maintain the faith.

About another of your direct descendants, I have something even more unexpected to tell. Remember your errant son Michael – the rebel, the runaway, the improbable convert to Afrikaner Nationalism, the first of your descendants to break the taboo and marry a gentile? Remember the two sons she produced for him and how their existence was concealed from your widow? Well, one of those sons in due course produced a son of his own, who has himself since performed the strange, ever-recurring trick of growing up. This young man is by descent one-quarter Jewish only (strange arithmetic, I grant you), and in religious terms (your religious terms) not remotely Jewish. But on what has he set his heart? What else but to undergo a conversion to orthodox Judaism, and, when he has completed that process, to enter a *yeshiva*. In other words, his ambition is to become a member of precisely the kind of institution from which (to your sorrow, in your dying years) your son Michael fled. Twice.

So much for our power to predict the future of those closest to us, let alone of nations and empires. So much, also, for our capacity to distinguish continuities from what may in fact be disruptions; or vice versa.

Here is another case for you to consider. The father of the young man I have just described is no longer alive. Like you, he died in his early fifties. Like you, of heart disease.

And here is yet another. Among the rest of your great-grandchildren whose jobs are known to me can be found a lawyer, a UN official, a research engineer, a doctor in general practice, an accountant, a specialist in Far Eastern marketing surveys, the editor of a photographic journal, a professional artist, two youth or community workers, a writer of television scripts, several teachers, and no less than six academic social scientists.

The Second World War was entirely of Hitler's making. If other great powers bore any responsibility for its outbreak, it was because they did not try to put a stop sooner to his successive acts of aggression: first in the Rhineland, then in Austria, the Czech Sudetenland and the rest of Czechoslovakia. Finally, with a hopeless belatedness, Britain and France reacted to his invasion of Poland. Less than a year later his armies had occupied Norway, Denmark, Belgium, Luxembourg, the Netherlands and France. Still he could not desist. He had to turn on the Soviet Union too. That, for him, had always been the real prize. Only through conquests in the east could he fulfil his dreams of acquiring *Lebensraum* for the German people and establishing a perpetual overlordship over 'inferior' races like the Poles and Russians. Only there, too, would he be able to capture the great majority of Europe's Jews and set about the task of killing them.

He made no secret of his intentions, as far as they were concerned. He declared repeatedly that this war (foisted on him by the Jews of course!) would end in their 'destruction', their 'annihilation'. His *Einsatzkommandos* went into action within days, even hours, of the invasion of the Soviet Union – which in itself reveals how diligently they had prepared themselves beforehand for the task. In the years that followed more and more men and ever greater material resources were devoted to the attaining of this objective; so were the more efficient methods of slaughter devised by German scientists, bureaucrats and industrialists. But the 'ultimate aim', the 'planned overall measures' which Heydrich, Himmler's second-in-command, had adumbrated almost two years before the invasion of the Soviet Union, remained unchanged.

Not even the Nazis, however, would have been able to persist with a campaign of premeditated, mechanized murder on so huge a scale, and across such distances, had their war by then not engaged more than the continent of Europe itself. When so many lives were being lost daily on all the battlefronts and behind them too, when entire cities and regions were being mutilated by wholesale acts of material destruction, when every form of censorship and propaganda was exercising its pressure on people in and out of uniform, and encouraging in them a sense of individual and national recklessness – in such circumstances who would know or care (the Nazis wished to believe) or would hold them responsible for what they and their helpers got up to in the woods of Lithuania or the plains of Poland? How many of their own people would dare to disobey the instructions given to them? Even if – or especially if – those who gave the instructions and those who carried them out knew them to be of an unprecedentedly criminal nature?

It is true that Stalin had not needed a world war in which to cloak his collectivizations, famines, purges, population transfers and labour camps. (Though he had the 'advantages' of being the heir of both war and revolution, and of ruling over an inaccessible empire far bigger than Europe itself.) Nor, like Hitler, did he lack for eager apologists abroad. More recently Mao Tse-tung's cataclysmic Great Leap Forward managed to find admirers at a distance too; so, though in much smaller numbers, did Pol Pot's massacres in Cambodia. (Nobody, as far as I know, has yet defended the recent slaughter of the Tutsis by the Hutus in Rwanda, perhaps because the latter failed to provide themselves with a grand ideology for what they were doing.) Beginning in ashen fantasy and demented power-lust, every reign of terror claims to be acting at the behest of an irresistible historical imperative; purporting to right the real or imaginary wrongs of the past, each promises to deliver to its followers a permanent control over the future. To mobilize their supporters to this end, such regimes have to wage war against enemies who are seen as both universally powerful and yet utterly contemptible; though not all define those enemies in outrightly racial or 'biological' terms, as the Nazis did.

So why, Heshel Melamed, after so many crimes larger or smaller in scope, some committed long ago, others taking place today, each one of which was or is as devastating to its victims as every other, why do I rake over these particular sorrows; why do I not let them go, and, in so doing, let you go too?

Well, I will end soon. But not before I have remarked on the singularities that marked out 'our' atrocity from all the others. Think of how embedded anti-Semitism, in all its interfused religious and racial forms, has hitherto been in the civilization of the West. Of the territorial and metaphysical unbounded-ness of the claims which it has always made for itself. Of the mechanical ingenuity and bureaucratic rationality of the Nazis' methods of killing people. (Merely starving and working them to death, as Stalin and Mao did with most of their victims, was too slow and unsensational for them.) Of the enormous difficulties they overcame to *find* people of every age and condition for the sole purpose of killing them. Of the distances they carried them in order to do it. Of the crazed relentlessness with which this *Judenjagd* was pursued when every other 'war aim' had long been given up.*

All of which brings me to speak of one other crime the Nazis committed, though you may be surprised that I should wish to mention it. I can best indicate its nature simply by pointing to the German people today. Think of the crime which the Nazis succeeded in getting their fathers and grandfathers to commit against *them*! Of course most Germans now, like most people everywhere, simply want to get on with their lives with as little discomfort as possible. If they are reminded of the events of more than fifty years ago, they are more likely than not to feel that the sufferings which their parents and grandparents went through had to 'cancel out', in some sense, what they did to others. Everyone knows too that there are corners of Germany in which Hitler is worshipped still and his fantasies nourished by assiduous haters, imbecile knowers of world secrets divulged to themselves alone. And in Germany and elsewhere – in Australia, the United States, Canada, various Latin American countries – there are German (and other) war criminals, old men once soaked in innocent blood, who in the same breath will deny that they ever did wrong and explain that they had no choice in the matter.

All that I take for granted. But I have met too many post-Hitler Germans not to know how deeply their consciousness of themselves has been scarred by shame, guilt and the half-hidden conviction that the people they belong to are never, as a people, to be wholly trusted; least of all by themselves. In their own eyes, and in this one respect, they have become what the Bible said the Israelites were: 'a people which stands alone'.

Judenjagd – 'Jew-hunt'. The word, commonly used by the German forces, seems to have been invented by them.

That is Hitler's legacy to them: the crime he persuaded one generation of Germans to commit against its successors.

Finally a word about South Africa: the country I left several decades ago in order to settle in England. Some of what I felt about it, and some of the reasons why I left it when I did, must already be apparent. I do not intend to enlarge on them here. What I do want to say is that the experience of growing up there has left me with an indelible impression of how strongly people feel the need to belong to identifiable groups – families, clans, associations, teams, tribes, nations, religions, even companies and corporations – which define themselves as much by the exclusion of others as they do by the cherishing of internal bonds between the members of each group. In other words, the sentiment of human solidarity is a reflex of another sentiment, to which I can only give the name of oppugnancy. We are no more able to experience the one without the other than we can expect to see youth without age or life without death. To pretend otherwise, on any grounds whatever, is just fatuous, if not positively insulting to the tormented course of human history as a whole.

If the sentiments of solidarity and oppugnancy are a part of our genetic make-up, as I am sure they are, we are also endowed with an extraordinary degree of adaptability and malleability, with a chameleon-like capacity to change our actions and attitudes, if not our predispositions, in accordance with changing circumstances and the demands of those placed in authority over us. Like our twin servitude to the passions of solidarity and oppugnancy, this kind of malleability or docility is also two-sided. Witness the large number of German soldiers who drove entire trainloads, whole towns and villages of unarmed men, women and children, to their places of execution, and then killed them at close range day after day, for months on end – not for the most part because they were (initially at any rate)

228

more cruel than other people, but because their officers ordered them to do it. By the same token, once the war was over most of them were able to go home and resume their lives as quiet, orderly, law-abiding citizens. Eichmann, no less, denied that he had ever been anti-Semitic. So did some of the figures more important than him who were tried at Nuremberg. Times had changed. They had changed. By now they genuinely believed that in their hearts they had always deplored the 'extreme measures' that had been carried out against the Jews. And if assertions of this kind could come from the mouths of former leaders of the Nazi Party, then how much more harmless, how much more to be pitied (by themselves, if not by anyone else), were those who had merely looked the other way when Jews were beaten in the streets, or had taken goods from a Jewish shop which others had smashed open, or quietly moved into a flat that 'relocated' Jews had left empty behind them? Or consider those creatures, eager to make a good impression on their rulers, who put notices outside their towns and suburbs during the Hitler epoch saying NO JEWS WANTED HERE or THIS TOWN IS FREE OF JEWS. When the war was over and they had counted their dead, they went back to their towns and suburbs – and lo and behold, the signs had disappeared (so had the Jews); the people who put them up had thrown away their Nazi Party badges; whatever they might still have said in the bosoms of their families, they now declared in public that they had never been Nazis really and what a pity it was that Hitler had 'exploited' their longing to see a 'regenerated' Germany.

Look what is happening in South Africa today. (In drawing the parallel I am not saying that South Africa was ever a Nazi state, for all the crimes committed by the government and its supporters during the apartheid years.) Most whites in South Africa today would find it difficult to comprehend the quasi-religious sense of outrage felt by earlier generations of people exactly like themselves at the prospect of sharing a bus or train compartment with a black man, or of shaking his hand, or of drinking with him in the same bar; let alone of having their children attend the same school or go to the same lavatory as his. And as for the idea of having him live in the house next door, or of seeing him in a position of authority in the workplace or sportsfield or parliament – ! That anyone should even think such things possible was itself an affront to nature, to God, to the way the world was made.

Today they happen all the time. It is largely taken for granted that they should do so, even by those whites who are deeply unhappy about the turn that their history has taken. When they are with family or friends, or in their favourite pub or at their sports club, they do not hide how sick it makes them feel. The warmth of solidarity fills their breast at every agreeing nod they see, at every assenting murmur they hear. If they go home and encounter the dark-skinned neighbour who has moved in not long before, their minds and bodies crawl with oppugnancy. But there is not much that they can do about it. The police will no longer come, as they would have done in the good old days of apartheid and the Group Areas Act, to chuck the man out of his house. Nor can they confidently expect, as they might once have done, that a randomly assembled crowd of their fellow whites will gladly help them do it.

So they have adapted. They try to get on with what is left of their lives on the best terms they can, in the context of the time and the circumstances in which they now live. They know themselves to be white men still, innately superior, and by a long way, to anyone of a darker skin colour than their own. But religious-moral fervour? A sense of the other's presence as an unbearable affront? The drunkenness of a murderous zeal against him?

Not any more. Not until next time. Not until a radical change of circumstances takes place, a different government comes into power, a war breaks out perhaps. Then . . .

I am sure, Heshel Melamed, you know what I mean.

PART FIVE

Never

[20]

Imagine swimming in a fluid which is all movement and light as you stroke your way through it, but which petrifies instantly behind you into granite cliffs and peaks, never to be shifted or altered by human effort.

Time is like that fluid. Like that granite. We swim through it for as long as we can, each of us adding our share to the Himalayan weights and fixities that at once assemble themselves behind us. Only in dreams, sometimes, is there a relenting. Just as the laws of gravity can be suspended in dreams, when we find ourselves able to fly simply by stretching out our arms, so the barbaric impenetrability of the past can suddenly begin to melt, to yield, to accommodate itself to a power we did not know we possessed.

So I end with a recent dream: one which showed, perhaps, that I had been guiltily brooding over my disinclination to go exploring for the possible site of my grandfather's *shul* and the family home during the last minutes of my visit to Varniai. The dream was straightforward (for a dream) and it will not take me long to tell it. Perhaps its most dreamlike feature was that the incredulity I felt throughout it was indistinguishable from the feeling that everything around me was also perfectly natural, homelike, tractable.

I was walking down a sandy road. I knew it to be in Varniai, as one knows such things in dreams, though nothing around me resembled what I had seen there. It was a dryer, browner, sparser place, in a different country, or perhaps in a different season. The soil was paler in colour too. There were wooden cottages which had neglected gardens in front of them: some were facing the road, others turned away from it. Behind them were the 'wrong' kind of trees: they looked like gum trees, with thin leaves and long, incurled strips of bark peeling away and hanging down their trunks. No one was about, but there was nothing alarming or sinister about my solitude. It could have been any time of day. The light was clear.

Then I came to the house. I knew it at once, though even as I recognized it I thought, 'She was wrong; it isn't double-storeyed; it isn't made of brick.' But it did have brick steps going up to the porch. There was a lightweight door of gauze in front of the main door, to keep out insects, in the South African fashion of many years ago. A moment later, though the door had not opened, I was no longer alone. I was in the middle of a group of children whom I knew to be my mother's brothers and sisters. Yet they were my children too; or at least I felt about them as I remembered feeling about my own children at that age: the same tenderness, amusement, anxiety. They smiled at me in the kindest manner, saying my name not to me but to each other, in explanatory fashion. Rather to my disappointment, their clothes were ordinary; not 'foreign', not 'period' at all. Their faces, however, were unfamiliar. Which of them was which? Who was who? How many of them were there? Where was my mother? Trying to think what I should call them, I found myself looking directly at a woman in early middle age who had joined the others as effortlessly and invisibly as they had gathered themselves around me. I could not tell if she was my mother or their mother or what the difference would be. She looked so young, so unlike any memory I had of either, I felt my heart would break. Someone was missing, though. I did not know how to speak of him and did not dare to ask where he was.

She understood anyway. She took my hand between both of hers – they were warm and dry, smooth and heavy – and calmly began to lead me into the house. There was no Hitler, no years, no Holocaust, no loss, no migration, no sorrow, everything was as it had been and always would be.

References and Notes

PART ONE: Lithuania

page **18** two conscientious encyclopedists of such communities: Nancy and Stuart Schoenburg, *Lithuanian Jewish Communities* (New York, 1991), p. 375.

page **27** to have borne yet another name: See entry on Trishick, *ibid*., p. 314. In the entry on Varniai in that volume (p. 375), my grandfather appears twice: first as Yisrael Yehoshua Segal, who is said to have been 'connected by marriage to Rabbi Zvi Yakov Oppenheim of Kelme' and to have died in 1910; then he is resurrected as Yehoshua Heshel Melamed, who assumed the rabbi's office in Varniai after the death of his 'predecessor'. But the two are the same man; and the connection by marriage to Rabbi Oppenheim arose through his second marriage, to Menuchah, my grandmother, who was one of the latter's three daughters.

Many years ago I wrote an article which referred to some members of my mother's family (*Commentary*, 75, 1, 1983, pp. 32–42). It produced an indignant letter from Long Island, New York, in which an elderly second cousin, herself from the 'old country', tried to put me right about my grandfather's change of name. Confirming that his surname had been 'Segal', her letter went on:

[Your grandmother] was widowed during the First World War. She was very young and had nine or ten children. Her sister-in-law, who lived in South Africa, offered the family a home, and [to] 'adopt' the children if she would come to live there and take the name of Melamed. Thereafter the name did become Segal-Melamed.

The trouble with this is that barely a word of it is true. We did not have any relatives in South Africa who went by the name of 'Melamed'; neither my mother nor any of her siblings ever referred to this mysterious benefactor whose name they had supposedly been compelled to take; nobody in the family ever used the name 'Segal-Melamed'. Anyway, I have in my possession a tattered identity document issued to my grandfather by the Russian authorities in 1908 – eleven years before his death and twelve years before the departure of his widow and children for South Africa. In this document his name is already given as Melamed, *tout court*. The fact that another branch of the family nurtured an elaborate, fictitious tale about his change of name might go to confirm my father's hunch that there was something dodgy about it – dodgy, that is, even by the standards of the time and place.

page 37 'During World War I the Jews left': N. and S. Schoenburg, *Lithuanian Jewish Communities*, p. 375.

page 38 'the entire Jewish population of those districts': Israel Cohen, *Vilnius* (Philadelphia, 1941), p. 359.

page 40 'blue eyes and delicate features': Private letter from Sadie Festenstein. My aunt's letter goes on, 'Incidentally, his genes are responsible for the auburn hair your mother had, and also our sister Rachel.'

PART TWO: South Africa

page 59 made their way to Cape Town: The figures in these paragraphs have been taken from various sources: e.g. the articles on 'Lithuania', 'South Africa' and 'United States of America' in *The Jewish Encyclopaedia* (1971); the articles on 'Lithuania' and 'The United States of America' in the *Encyclopaedia Britannica* (1963 edition); Gustav Saron and Louis Hotz, *The History of the Jews in South Africa*

(Oxford, 1957); Masha Greenbaum, *The Jews of Lithuania* (Tel Aviv, 1995); *Lithuania: A Short Guide* (Vilnius, 1994).

page 59 during this period went to South Africa: Of course not all these 'Russian' immigrants remained in South Africa. Many returned to Lithuania or Latvia; others eventually left for North America. Among the latter group, strangely enough, were the fathers of two of America's leading contemporary novelists, Saul Bellow and Norman Mailer.

page 60 'among the Lithuanian peasants': Saron and Hotz, *The History of the Jews in South Africa*, p. 69.

page 61 'for the restoration of its synagogue': *Ibid.*, p. 73.

page 62 ambitions of many of his fellow countrymen: *Ibid.*, pp. 194–5. M. D. Hersch 'expressed unqualified sympathy for the Boer Republic [in its struggles against Britain's imperial designs] and dwelt on the freedom and economic opportunities enjoyed by the Jewish new-comers'.

page 65 'which grain will grow and which will not': *Macbeth* I.iii. 58–9.

page 77 the Russian Jewish poet: *The Prose of Osip Mandelstam*, translated and edited by Clarence Brown (Princeton, 1965), pp. 79, 82. Though his father originally came from Latvia, Mandelstam himself was brought up in pre-Bolshevik St Petersburg. He too eventually perished in a concentration camp: one of Stalin's in his case, not Hitler's.

page 91 if they could have reached us: On the dissemination of the first reports of the wholesale destruction of European Jewry, see Walter Laqueur, *The Terrible Secret* (London, 1980), pp. 72 *et seq.* On the Nazis' plans for the extermination of those Jewish communities which had not yet fallen into their hands, see Martin Gilbert, *The Holocaust: The Jewish Tragedy* (London, 1987), pp. 280–81. At the notorious Wannsee Conference in December 1942, Reinhold Heydrich, Himmler's second-in-command in the SS, had no hesitation in including among his 'targets' the (so far) unattainable Jewish communities of such countries as Turkey, Switzerland, Sweden, Great Britain, Portugal and the Irish Republic.

page 92 had lost its éclat even for them: The Afrikaner Nationalists came to power only after Hitler had been defeated. This was just as well for them – not to speak of everyone else in the country – though it did not restrain them from elaborating and viciously intensifying the patterns of racial segregation and discrimination they had inherited.

Paradoxically, a similar degree of unwanted good fortune attended the coming to power of the current rulers of the country, the African National Congress. Success came to them only after their backers and ideological inspirers in the Soviet Union had lost the Cold War and the Soviet empire had disintegrated.

page 96 *The Electronic Elephant: A Southern African Journey* (London, 1994).

page 97 the poet Edward Thomas: 'The New House' in *Collected Poems* (London, 1951), p. 123.

PART THREE: Lithuania

page 124 were alive four years later: Rachel Kostanian, *The Jewish State Museum of Lithuania* (Vilnius, 1996), p. 19.

page 125 'liquidated in similar fashion': *Encyclopaedia of the Holocaust*, Vol. II (New York, 1990), p. 898.

page 125 'solving the Jewish problem in Lithuania': Gilbert, *The Holocaust*, p. 234.

page 125 and then shot: *Ibid.*, p. 230.

page 126 for hundreds of miles around: Even the exclamation mark after *Geheime Reichsache* tells one something of Jaeger's pride in what he was to call, in his 1 December report, 'this nerve-scraping work' (*ibid.*, pp. 234–5). The self-pity in that phrase merely emphasizes the sense of accomplishment conveyed by his report. Many others among the murderers felt deeply sorry for themselves, from time to time. SS Colonel Paul Blobel, a roving expert not only on mass murder but also on mass cremation, actually remarked on one occasion that his men 'suffered more from nervous exhaustion than those who were to be shot' (Leon Poliakov, *Harvest of Hate* [New

York, 1954], p. 130). Another officer who boasted of the 'ruthless sweeps' his unit was making, and whose massacres of men, women and children were no less extensive than Jaeger's, wrote to a superior officer about how hard it was for him, *as a married man* (my italics), to be deprived of the company of his wife and 'my Dieter and my little Lina' (*ibid.*, p. 128). Christopher Browning's *Ordinary Men* (New York, 1992) gives the best account known to me of how men of lower rank in the killing units, including many who were initially horrified to learn what their 'duties' were, soon became inured to the task, or even enthusiastic about it. Browning also shows that the few who remained obdurate in their refusal to take part in the shootings generally went unpunished – aside from having to put up with the scorn of their companions.

page 127 still in my possession: See note to page 27 and the reference to this document on page 13.

page 130 or any other like it: On the attempts to keep the massacres secret, see Raul Hilberg, *The Destruction of the European Jews*, Vol. 2 (Chicago, 1985), pp. 322 *et seq.*, in which the document referring to 'decency and discipline' is quoted. See also Gerald Reitlinger, *The Final Solution: The Attempt to Exterminate the Jews of Europe, 1939–1945* (London, 1953), pp. 199–200. Gilbert (*The Holocaust*, p. 198) refers to two German soldiers who were sentenced to a year's imprisonment apiece for having 'taken snapshots' of a massacre in Uman, Poland.

Newspaper reports published late in 1996 have confirmed that within a few weeks of the opening of the war on the eastern front British Intelligence had become aware of the scale of the killings by the *Einsatzkommandos* and other units in some regions of Poland and Russia. This information was not made public, it is said, in order to keep the German high command ignorant of the fact that their codes had been broken. However, when news of the Final Solution did reach Allied and neutral countries from other sources, no effective or even ineffective response followed. Laqueur (*The Terrible Secret*, p. 208) writes:

No power could have saved the majority of the Jews of Eastern Europe and the Reich in the summer of 1942 ... After the winter of 1942 the situation rapidly changed: the satellite leaders and even some of the German officials were no longer eager to be accessories to mass murder. Some, at least, would have responded to Allied pressure, but such pressure was never exerted.

page 148 who so vastly outnumbered them: There were 7,000 Jews, Shlomo claimed, still living in Lithuania – though, since he also told me that the community in Kaunas now numbered only 700, I could not understand how he had arrived at this figure. My own experience, like that of many other visitors to Lithuania, would suggest that there is hardly a Jewish soul left in the countryside; and even if one assumes that there were three or four times as many Jews in Vilnius as in Kaunas, and adds a few hundred extra for Klaipeda (Memel), the country's third-largest city, the total would still fall short of the number Shlomo gave to me. The most common estimate for the Jewish population of Lithuania at the time of the German invasion in 1941 is a quarter of a million – a figure which includes the tens of thousands who had fled there from German-occupied Poland. Of those who survived the war (most of them did so by fleeing with the retreating Russian army), many left for Israel in the 1970s, when the Communist government began granting exit visas to that country.

page 150 *Pan Tadeusz*, translated by Kenneth Mackenzie (London, 1964). Sections of the poem have also been translated by Donald Davie under the title *The Forests of Lithuania* (Hessle, Yorkshire, 1959).

page 151 *Native Realm*, translated by Catherine S. Leach (London, 1968).

page 157 *Surviving the Holocaust: The Kovno Ghetto Diary of Avraham Tory*, edited by Martin Gilbert (London, 1991), pp. 8, 11.

page 161 done to so many others: Gilbert (*The Holocaust*, p. 678) quotes an account by a Lithuanian witness to the shooting of the French prisoners. It appears that they were murdered not in the field outside the fort but in the courtyard described at the beginning of this chapter, after they had tried to seize the guns of their killers.

Hannah Arendt's remark about Himmler is taken from her *Eichmann in Jerusalem: A Report on the Banality of Evil* (London, 1963), p. 125.

page 164 A *kompromis*: After referring to the 'savagery' of Lithuanian and Latvian bands, Reitlinger (*The Final Solution*, pp. 213–14) goes on to write of 'whole regiments of Lithuanian police and *Selbstschutz* [used] to guard the camps and ghettos, to run the concentration centres, and to cut down cringing old people and children during the "actions"'.

Also Greenbaum (*The Jews of Lithuania*, p. 341):

It is difficult to understand the reason for the extreme violence that so many Lithuanians perpetrated against their Jewish neighbours, with whom they had lived in comparative peace for so long . . . Lithuanian Jews had rarely suffered the indignities of the pogroms that were so common in Poland and Russia. Yet in 1941, as soon as the Red Army pulled out of Lithuania, even before the German forces arrived, pogroms that claimed thousands of lives erupted . . . From the time the Nazis arrived until the moment they left, Lithuanians helped them implement the Final Solution in the ghettos, the forts, and the labour camps. They proved so effective in their work that they were organized into special Lithuanian battalions dispatched to other areas of the eastern front for similar killing operations.

page 166 look around you: In *Eichmann in Jerusalem* Hannah Arendt famously makes play with the idea of the 'banality of evil'. For all her apparent sophistication, she shows an extraordinary blindness to the perverted ambitions which actually helped to motivate and sustain Eichmann and innumerable others, both above and below him in rank. It simply never occurs to her that in committing their terrible crimes, and as a result of having committed them, they became convinced that ordinariness, banality, the realm of the commonplace, was precisely what they had for ever left behind. They had 'transcended' it.

page 172 'A dozen folk could sup as in a room?': Mickiewicz, *Pan Tadeusz*, trans. Mackenzie, Book 3, p. 76.

page 178 'any display of antisemitism': Quoted in Greenbaum, *The*

Jews of Lithuania p. 343. See the reference in Chapter 10 to the portrait of President Landsbergis's mother, which hangs among the pictures of Righteous Gentiles in the Jewish State Museum in Vilnius.

page 178 all over eastern Europe: See note to page 164.

page 208 a collection of such photographs: Assembled by Ephraim Oshry (New York and Montreal, 1951), no page numbers.

PART FOUR: Now

page 225 their 'destruction', their 'annihilation': Lucy S. Dawidowicz, *The War Against the Jews 1933–45* (London, 1987), pp. 143, 147–8.

page 225 remained unchanged: Gilbert, *The Holocaust*, pp. 88–9.

page 227 *Judenjagd*: Browning, *Ordinary Men*, p. 123. Under neither *Jude* nor *Jagd* is the word recorded in the large Collins/Klett *German–English Dictionary* (London and Stuttgart, 1981).